AdSense

The Behavioral Science of Advertising

Kirk Donovan

ISBN: 1-4140-3551-9 (e-book)
ISBN: 1-4140-3550-0 (Paperback)

Library of Congress Control Number: 2003099291

This book is printed on acid free paper.

Printed in the United States of America
Bloomington, IN

1stBooks – rev. 02/13/04

This book is dedicated to all the wonderful people I have met, worked with and taught in the amazing world of advertising. I have learned from all of them, and I hope they have learned something from me. I could not have found a more rewarding and satisfying career.

Introduction

What do you think of advertising? That's a question I have asked people for over 20 years and the answers are usually the same. People don't like advertising. They don't feel like they're influenced by it. Advertising is intrusive and unwelcome. Unless, of course, it's strongly emotional or very funny, like the old long distance telephone company ads. Remember those? The ones with the little sweet grandmother, in tears because she got a call from a grandson overseas that she hasn't heard from in months. Very emotional music, very touching message. *Reach out and touch.*

Each generation has their "memorable" ads. The little old lady eating the hamburgers and beckoning "Where's the beef?!" Plop plop, fizz fizz, oh what a relief it is! Or those great beer ads, from Budweiser to Miller Light? The classic animated frogs and salamanders doing verbal battle in front of a big neon Budweiser sign.

How many people do you know turn on television to watch the ads? Have you heard of any successful radio stations that broadcast 24 hours a day with commercials only? And why do newspapers have all those stories around the ads?

It doesn't mean we're <u>consciously</u> aware of each message. We are probably cognizant of very few of them, but they are ever-present. But are we <u>influenced</u> by them? If so, which ones? Why do some work and some do not? What does it take to make advertising successful?

Early to bed, early to rise,
work like Hell and advertise.

--Ted Turner

Table of Contents

Chapter One
The Global Village

The global village, as defined by Marshall McLuhan, has evolved into a fierce competition for business. The big devour the small. Mom and Pop had to retire. The survival of the fittest has helped define business success, and even the successful businesses have no guarantees of continued success. Many of the mighty fall each year. Even advertising greats like CBS Television, once called the "Tiffany Network," suffered a great downfall in the 1990s.

Do you think advertising money is wasted? If a survey was done among all the business owners who read this book, you would see some startling results. Ask them if they feel like they've ever wasted money on advertising. I guarantee 99% of them would say yes. Ask them if they've figured out what makes advertising effective. I guarantee most of them would say no. That is why they are reading this book.

Remember Charlie the Tuna, the lovable spoke*fish* for Starkist? Where is he today? In that big casserole in the sky! He had a good job for a long time, but eventually the public no longer found him cute.

And what about the cute Chihuahua that led Taco Bell into the 21st century? He had his 15 minutes of fame, but produced no results for the fast food giant.

Why do you think these loveable characters are unemployed now? Because even successful campaigns don't stay successful forever. Why? Because we are <u>fickle</u>. The more repetitious the message becomes, the more resilient it becomes. Increased audience awareness of competition decreases brand loyalty.

The Big Picture

According to U.S. Census Bureau statistics, over 65% of all business in this country will fail in five years. And over half of those failures will happen in the first year! Annually, thousands of people lose everything they've ever worked for in a disappointing business collapse. And they all had one thing in common when they began their businesses. They all had the glow of confidence and total belief that what they were doing had every chance for success. Not a single one anticipated failure.

Billions of dollars are invested in advertising every year. Nearly 85% of that advertising is either not effective at all, or not as effective as it could be. That accounts for a lot of wasted money. Advertising is a multi-billion dollar industry. Why does 85% fail? This book will focus on some of the reasons. It will give those who have wasted money on advertising an entirely new perspective.

Advertisers, and those who make the ads, must learn this new perspective in order to potentially reduce waste. We will explore the "big picture" of how products are marketed, and the impact it has on our society.

This book can't guarantee you more success in your future advertising endeavors. But developing a new perspective of the <u>purpose</u> of advertising will give you a definite edge in the battle for the minds of your potential customers.

Through this book, I can't tell you how your business in Sioux City, Iowa can develop an advertising campaign that will fall into the 15% that succeeds. That would take a personal analysis of your business and your marketplace, your competitors, the current economic conditions and much more.

What I <u>will</u> show you in these pages, though, are many of the reasons why 85% of it fails. Hopefully, with that knowledge, you will reduce your chances of falling into that ominous percentage of wasted dollars.

Kirk Donovan

I have discovered the most exciting, the most arduous literary form of all, the most difficult to master, the most pregnant in curious possibilities.... I mean the advertisement. It is far easier to write ten effective Sonnets than one effective advertisement that will take in a few thousand of the uncritical buying public.

Aldous Huxley— "On the Margin'

Kirk Donovan

Chapter Two
My Mother Was A Story Lady

My mother was a story-lady. She worked at a radio station in upstate New York, and hosted a show for children. I vaguely recall memories of sitting in my bunk bed with my sister, Vicki, listening to my mother tell sweet stories and sing songs.

My father also worked in radio. He was a deep voiced, smooth-sounding newscaster for the Mutual Broadcasting Network back in the late 1940s.

My first radio job was host of a radio show on a small FM station on the campus of Claremont Men's College in Claremont, California. It was the summer between my junior and senior years in high school.

My best friend Greg Gatling and I hosted a one hour show every Saturday at 6 p.m. on K.C.M.C., the "voice of the four colleges in Claremont, California…880 on the AM dial, 90.1 on the FM dial."

It was called "The Kirk and Greg Comedy Hour," a compilation of our own comedy skits and segments of comedy albums from legends of the day like Bob Newhart, Bill Cosby and Jonathan Winters. It was probably the lamest show in broadcasting, two young teens giggling and having fun. And we got paid for it! Twenty-five dollars a week. It was the starting point of a successful career. As you can see, I started at the very bottom!

After high school, I enlisted in the U.S. Air Force, served a tour of duty in Viet Nam and finished my military career at Eglin Air Force Base in Florida. I was on my own and destined for a career in radio. On the day of my discharge, I boarded a bus and journeyed to Mobile, Alabama. It was in the early 1970s.

Those were the days that you were required to have a 3rd class broadcast license from the Federal Communications Commission in order to be on the air. I studied the F.C.C. manual feverishly on the bus to Mobile, and passed the test.

In early January I walked into W.F.S.H., a tiny 250 watt radio station in Niceville, Florida. It had an audience of about a dozen people, on a good day! Even worse, I started on the overnight shift. Thus began an illustrious career in a continuously changing industry, a career that covered over a decade.

From Niceville, I moved up to the "big leagues," the top 40 AM station in the Gulf Coast community of Fort Walton Beach, Florida. I worked the overnight shift again, but this was a 1000-watt station! It covered the whole city!

After seeing and believing in my abilities, my mentor, Gabby Bruce, program director for WNUE Radio, moved me to the daytime shift. My career continued to blossom.

I worked for a fun radio station in a tourist town. I was having the time of my life. I was developing a "voice" and a "delivery." I was learning a new business. There was only one problem. The money!

It was difficult for a young kid to survive back then making just $100 a week. And you couldn't put "fun" in the refrigerator.

Go Where the Money Is

I loved being on the air, but my ambitions went beyond announcing. Very early in my career, I understood that the success of the station depended on advertising revenue. That was instilled by my mother, who always said that I'd never make any money on the air. "The money is in sales," she said emphatically and repeatedly.

So, beginning from those early days on WFSH Radio, I would come back to the radio station every afternoon and wait for the salespeople to return with notes for new commercials. These scribbled notes came on the back of restaurant receipts, napkins, business cards, even inside the cover of matchbooks.

I spent my time hanging around the salespeople more than my fellow announcers, asking questions, going on sales calls, being a general nuisance.

I would volunteer to write the commercials, a chore most of the salespeople hated. I knew nothing about writing commercials, but neither did the salespeople. In most cases, they were happy to turn the responsibility over to me.

After two years of announcing, I decided that in order to make more money, I needed to sell advertising on a commission basis. So one hungry afternoon I ventured into the sales manager's office and proclaimed I was ready to start selling advertising.

By that time, I had developed enough of an "announcer voice" that selling ads was easy. I would meet a potential advertiser, try to sell him on the merits of my radio station, and then in front of the prospect, write a few cute lines about his business. And I had a trick. I would always incorporate the potential client's name somewhere in the commercial. I would then read his script in my interesting-yet-undeveloped voice.

"So come see Bob Smith today, and see what he can do for you!"

It was a useful advantage, and constantly produced the highest billings of any other salesperson on the staff. Once the client heard their name in an announcer voice, it usually closed the sale. Most salespeople didn't have that advantage. Most of them didn't have the voice, and most of them couldn't think creatively on their feet.

Through the early days of my career, I wrote literally hundreds of commercials. Some worked very well. The customers got good results and continued to buy the station. I kept my job. But, as you probably noticed, I said "some" of them worked. A lot more of them <u>didn't</u> work. And I didn't understand why. I spent much more time agonizing over the ads that didn't work than languishing in the glory of those that did.

It was very frustrating and perplexing to spend hours creating what I thought was the ideal commercial, only to have it fail. Some even won industry awards. They sounded good, but they just didn't get results for the client.

At other times, I would get back to the radio station with copy that needed to go on the air the same day. In a panic, I would write a quick script, run into the production room and throw it together with minutes to spare. The results? A lot of times they were exceptional.

Why did <u>those</u> spots work while the others failed? What made people respond to some commercials and not to others? The answer created the foundation for my career.

Kirk Donovan

In the last couple of weeks I have seen the ads for Wonder Bra. Is that really a problem? Men not paying enough attention to women's breasts?!

--Jay Leno

Kirk Donovan

Chapter Three
Advertising--A Behavioral Science

After five years of radio announcing and selling advertising, I moved to Tallahassee, Florida, to attend Florida State University. I worked my way through college as a full time radio salesperson at a local radio station.

Upon completion of my Bachelors Degree in Speech Communication, I decided to continue my academic career. There were several degree programs from which I could choose, including public relations, advertising, even marketing. All seemed to be logical progressions to my aspiring advertising career. But at that point, after five years of questioning the effects of advertising, I chose to pursue the study of behavioral science. The degree program was called *Interpersonal Communication*.

It was a relatively new field of study, the academic marriage of psychology and sociology. I wanted to learn what makes people behave, what makes them respond to certain things and not to others. At that point in my career, I had learned that the purpose of advertising could be defined very simply. The reason a business spends any money on advertising is to get people to <u>respond</u>. It's really that simple.

After graduating summa cum laude with a Master's Degree, I studied for two more years toward a PhD in a specially designed program called Interpersonal Communication. Experientially I was learning advertising. Academically I was becoming a behavioral scientist.

Are you a behavioral scientist? Believe it or not, you are. How old are you? How long have you been behaving? You are a behavioral scientist because you have behaved all your life. And you have observed behavior your entire life. All I did through academia was to learn the "language" of behavioral science. But you have a base understanding of it. Throughout this book, I will tap into that innate understanding, and ask you to use it in analyzing the many aspects of advertising.

A Bumpy Ride

Playing the advertising game is somewhat like playing poker with your money. When you play poker, you may win some of the time, but you would also lose some of the time. If you took a course on how to play poker from a leading expert, you'd learn more about the strategy of poker playing, and chances are you would win more. But you certainly wouldn't win every time.

Now, if you knew absolutely nothing about advertising and you decided to buy a radio or television campaign, or run an advertisement in a local newspaper, chances are you would get someone to respond to the message, depending on what you are trying to get across in the ad. But what do you think are the odds of that ad being successful? Probably pretty slim.

The more you advertise, and the more you learn <u>how</u> to advertise, the chances are good that you'll be successful more often, depending on how much money you have to lose trying to learn.

But if you learn the business of advertising, and if you learn what makes people <u>respond</u> to messages, your chances of falling into the 85% of advertising that fails is greatly diminished. Or, better stated, your chances for success are much better.

But will it work every time? Probably not, because it's still poker.

There are so many conditions that could lead to a failed campaign…the weather, the economy, the competition, the location… the list goes on. All you can do is try to understand some of the reasons why most advertising fails and reduce your chances for failure. But you still have to figure out what will work for <u>you</u> and your business. That takes an understanding of marketing, advertising and behavioral science.

What I <u>will</u> offer in this book is a behavioral scientist's impressions of why 85% of all advertising is either ineffective or not as effective as it could be. In addition, you'll learn through the perspective of a veteran of advertising sales, who started on the streets at the smallest of stations and built an extremely successful career.

With those two perspectives, you could be well on your way

to <u>not</u> wasting money. But there are many obstacles ahead. Some are based on external conditions over which we have little control.

A lot of obstacles, though, are caused by internal senses of what we *think* advertising should do, based mostly on our observations as consumers. So often those senses blind the reality of what advertising really <u>should</u> do, and our expectations are inflated.

Advertising is the foot on the accelerator, the hand on the throttle, the spur on the flank that keeps our economy surging forward.

--Robert W. Sarnoff

Kirk Donovan

Chapter Four
The Uphill Climb

I want to spend some time telling you about the uphill climb that advertising has to overcome in its pursuit of success. And it _is_ an enormous climb, with many obstacles.

My family told me a story about my late father that took place during his youth. He spent a career in advertising and had the creative mind of an advertising genius. He was always thinking about ways to get messages across. When he was a 17-year-old, living in Oklahoma, he ventured off with a friend to vacation in Mexico.

On the way back, they ran short of money outside Amarillo. It was 1927 and Amarillo was a small desert town on the plains of Texas. In town that week was a traveling circus. My father, scheming on how to get the finances to return home, came across the circus manager. He offered to parade the circus elephant through the streets of Amarillo with two huge signs strapped over it promoting the Big Tent Event.

For his hot afternoon of walking that pachyderm through town, he earned enough money to get back to Oklahoma. It was his first advertising commission. Times have changed. The messages have changed, and thankfully, so have the messengers.

The Over Communicated Society

Are you aware of how deeply advertising permeates our daily lives? Think about it. Probably one of the first things you see every single morning is a logo on your tube of toothpaste, and on your deodorant. At least the people getting anywhere near you that day hope so.

Then, a lot of you see the logo on your coffee can or cereal box, and you browse through ads as you rush through the newspaper, and you hear ads on your favorite morning radio station on the way to work. You drive behind a Ford logo on the back of a truck, pass dozens of billboards and signage with other recognizable logos of several businesses, and walk past a guy with a Nike logo on his shoes and an Izod alligator on his shirt. And it's only 9 a.m.!

Believe it or not, we're bombarded with over 1500 advertising impressions every single day. When you brush your teeth, that logo on the toothpaste is an advertising impression. And the one on your coffee can, and the logo on the truck in front of you on the way to work, and all the billboards and signage you pass by, and all the radio and TV ads and computer ads!!

This has been happening since each of us was a child. If you're 30 years old, you've been exposed to 16,425,000 messages. That's enough to give you a headache. After a while, it becomes very **redundant**. We <u>are</u> the over-communicated society!

In addition, the words of the ads are mostly rhetorical. How many messages have told you how great a product was, or that it was new, or improved, or bigger, or best or friendliest? And how often have you been disappointed?

We hear about the wonderful performance of an on-time airline, but every time we fly it, it gets to our destination late. A bank's advertising focuses on their "friendly" staff, the ones who "treat you special." But how many of the tellers end up making eye contact and smiling at you? Especially at noon on the 15th of the month, when the lines keep getting longer!

The concept of fast food restaurants began midway through the 20th century with two common messages: <u>fast</u> and <u>friendly</u>. But today, most of them have lost touch with both promises. They hire young kids who, even if they *could* say "thanks for your order…I hope you have a wonderful day," are not trained to say it with a smile on their face. Most of the time, they can't even get the simple order correct. Sounds cynical, but go order a hamburger and see if you don't get a chicken sandwich!

And what about restaurants describing themselves as having the "best food in town," only to find when you get there that the soup is cold, the salad is soggy and the steak is full of fat? It happened to me last night!

You've been disappointed more than once, I'm sure. We don't

believe the rhetoric we hear or see anymore, because we've all been burned before.

Resilient Advertising Messages

So what happens when messages become redundant and rhetorical? They become **resilient**. That means we don't pay attention to them. They fall right off our attention bridge. That's very disconcerting to the person who just spent good money trying to get your attention.

Remember the uphill climb I mentioned? How do you like it so far? Unfortunately, we're nowhere near the summit. Another obstacle to penetrating the mind of your potential customer is that we don't usually go <u>looking</u> for advertising.

There are some advertising categories that we <u>are</u> conditioned to look for, though. In most communities, we know where to go if we want to see what's playing at the movie theater. We go to the entertainment section of the newspaper. If we're looking for a plumber, we usually "let our fingers do the walking" through the Yellow Pages. And where do we go to compare used car prices or to find grocery coupons? We all know the grocery coupons are in the local newspaper, because they fall out of the paper every Sunday morning! For some businesses, knowing <u>where</u> to advertise is a no-brainer.

But there aren't too many categories that afford such luxury.

How many people do you know who turn on the television to watch the commercials? Who rushes to their car every afternoon to hear their favorite radio ads? Who spends Sunday afternoons driving around looking for billboards?

And how many people love taking ten items out of their mailbox when only one is a letter from a loved one and the other nine are ads for carpet cleaning or C.D. collections? The average life expectancy of a direct mail piece in today's over-communicated society is from the time you get it out of your mailbox to the walking distance of the nearest garbage can. Millions of dollars are spent every year on this medium.

There are well over 50 times more products for each category than our parents had just 50 years ago. There are 50 times more choices in soft drinks. There are 50 times more choices in automobile brands, and soap powders and breakfast cereals. In the automobile business there are imports, exports, sport utility vehicles, trucks, small, large, fast, slow, luxurious and clunkers. If Henry Ford only knew what he started!

We do not like to be the recipients of advertising messages. I have conducted countless surveys over the years to determine how many people will admit that advertising influences them. The overwhelming answer is no, we are not influenced by it! Why? We've all been burned before.

So let's create a scenario. You and I own the best Italian restaurant in town. We hire an incredible chef, the warmest and friendliest employees and we have the best food and a truly unique ambiance. So we put our message into a nice radio ad.

"Come to Luigi's Italian Restaurant, the <u>best</u> Italian dining experience in town. You'll love our décor, our warm and friendly staff and our wonderful food."

Do the listeners believe it? Probably not. But we <u>are</u> the best in town! Sorry. The message is redundant, rhetorical and resilient.

"Yeah! We've heard <u>that</u> before!"

I've always told my students that probably the most difficult form of writing is poetry. I say that because poetry is one of the oldest forms of writing. Most poetry is written about emotions, and how many emotions <u>are</u> there? Too many to name.

But in reality, there are only a finite number of emotions. That means that humankind has been writing about essentially the same things for thousands of years.

So what is good poetry? It's writing about something that's been written about before, but saying it in a way that has never been said before. You don't want to plagiarize.

In writing good poetry, you must take all you want to say concerning a particular emotion and narrow it down into clear, short concise sentences in a way that triggers an emotional response. That's not easy to do.

Now let's compare poetry to advertising. A good advertising message usually talks about something that's been talked about before, because there aren't many products or services that have no competition. So you have to create a message about something other people have talked about before, but say it in a different way. Again, you don't want to plagiarize.

You have to consider everything you can possibly say to let the public know the good things about your product or service, and then narrow it down into 30 or 60 seconds, or squeeze it into a quarter page newspaper ad.

And you have to trigger an emotional response if you want any chance of making the message effective.

That's where poetry stops. Advertising requires something additional, something poetry doesn't require. To be successful, it must also trigger a behavioral response. You must get someone to act on your message. Sound difficult? It is. It's one of the major reasons why 85% of all advertising is not effective.

What Does Work?

What about the 15% of advertising that does work? It proves that advertising <u>can</u> be effective. Aside from the bleak picture I have painted about the uphill climb, there are so many indications that advertising is a powerful, motivating and dynamic influence on our society.

Up until about 75 or 80 years ago, colognes and perfumes were affordable only to the wealthy. And what about deodorant? It's been around about 75 years. That means that prior to about 75 or 80 years ago, throughout all of human history, our natural body odor was natural!

With the advent of mass communication and mass distribution, and with the help of advertising messages being pounded into our heads throughout the years that we have to <u>smell</u> good to be <u>attractive</u>, an entire industry was created. If we get near someone who exhibits natural body odor, we are offended. What was natural through all of history became unnatural in just 75 years.

Communication didn't just create a habit, it created an entire industry and it changed the olfactory sense, the sense of smell. And it happened in a relatively short period of time. Advertising is <u>indeed</u> a powerful influence for society.

So how do we figure out how to tap into that power? How do

we learn the ways to create advertising campaigns that work? First we have to identify the *purpose* of advertising.

Advertising is the greatest art form of the 20th Century.

Marshall McLuhan-Advertising Age - 1976

Kirk Donovan

Chapter Five
Purpose of Advertising

The first question that should be asked by anyone doing advertising is "What is the purpose for this?" That sounds like a simple question, but most people don't have a clue!

Most businesses advertise out of fear. "If I don't advertise, how will I compete with those in my industry that <u>do</u>?"

Many businesses advertise because they just think that's what they're <u>supposed</u> to do. And some advertise because they <u>like</u> to. They like to see their creation, or their mug, on the big screen or in print. There is a little Steven Spielberg in all of us.

After years in the advertising business, after countless hours of sales training, sales seminars, and reading just about every book I could ever find on the topic, I realized the purpose of advertising. If you have ever spent one dime on advertising, for yourself or someone else's business, there is just one purpose for the expenditure. That purpose is to get someone to <u>respond</u>.

That's it. It's that simple. All you can hope to do is get someone or a group of people on the other end of the advertisement to <u>respond</u> to your message.

There are any number of ways that the audience could respond.

The response could be a telephone call. It could be getting them in their car and driving to your location. The desired response could be as simple as remembering your name, or creating an impression of your business in their mind. It could be as simple as someone muttering "Hmmm."

What Response Do
I Want?

As I mentioned, there are a myriad of ways a person can respond. It can be an emotional response, a behavioral response, or it could be "stored" in a person's subconscious, where it can eventually be recalled…or slowly fade into the mind's abyss of lost impressions.

You must develop a sense of what you want the response to <u>be</u> before you do any media planning or creative planning.

How do you determine what response you want? It can't be as simple as "getting people through my doors!" If that is your desired response, you might as well just send them your money! What if you <u>do</u> get a lot of people in your door, but no one makes a single purchase? Were you happy with the response?

And the response can't be to just *sell* your product. You cannot sell with advertising. Selling must be done face to face.

Over the years, in seminars and in my business endeavors, I've asked business owners what they thought was the purpose of advertising. The answers varied as greatly as the businesses. Some said that advertising was supposed to "sell" their product. Then I would ask, "Do you know when selling starts?" There were many answers, but the simplest is the most logical. It starts when the prospect says no.

Consider the following scenario. Gus is a car salesman. Mary comes in and points out a car she heard about on the radio. "How much is it?" she asks. Gus responds "22,500." "I'll take it," Mary says.

Gus does the paperwork and hands Mary the keys to her new car. Did Gus make a sale? No. Gus just facilitated the paperwork. If Mary had said *no*, Gus would have to determine and answer her objections. That is when selling actually begins.

If you try to *sell* your product or service in an advertisement, and someone on the other end of the ad looks at it and says "no", you don't have the opportunity to change their mind. You didn't get their name, their e-mail address, their phone number or where they work. You never even saw them. But they saw you, and they weren't impressed. Too late to be able to do something about that first impression.

Besides, how can you sell anything in a 3x5" newspaper ad, or in a 60-second radio ad? If you try to sell in your advertising, the chances are great you will fall into the 85% of it that fails.

THE RESPONSE UMBRELLA

Let's open an umbrella. We'll call it our Response Umbrella. Underneath the umbrella there are many potential responses…but they're all some form of a response.

Under the guidelines of AdSense, there are basically three things you can do with an advertising message under that umbrella. You can <u>inform</u>. You can <u>entertain</u>. And you can <u>entice</u>. Which of these you attempt will determine the potential response.

Some business owners I have dealt with over the years had just one purpose in mind for their advertising. They just wanted the public to remember their name. Or they wanted to create an <u>image</u> of their product or service. This is called "institutional" advertising.

Ford Motor Company advertises the quality of their product and their people. Their ads *inform* us of new styles and innovations.

Political ads *inform* us about the positive attributes of a candidate, or the negatives about his opponent.

Coca Cola ads have always *entertained* us with pictures of the world at work and play, refreshing themselves with a cold beverage. Budweiser Beer ads entertained us with animated frogs chanting *Bud-weis-er.*

Sportswear has gotten to be a huge industry, making brands like *Reebok* and *Nike* household names. When I was growing up, I asked for tennis shoes. Today, my kids want a pair of "Nikes." But do the national Nike ads tell you where to buy your shoes ? No, they are just entertaining ads, mostly showing sports stars wearing their shoes or hats or shirts. In many cases, out of a 30 second ad, you don't even know who the message is <u>for</u> until the last 3 or 4 seconds, when they show their logo.

So, ads can inform and they can entertain. The other purpose of advertising is to *entice.* To entice is to elicit a physical, behavioral response.

The Budweiser or Coca-Cola ads don't say anywhere in the ads that you should go get one. In most cases, they don't even suggest <u>where</u> to go. It just leaves an impression.

The national Ford ad doesn't say, "Go out and buy this Ford." It doesn't tell you which Ford dealer to go to, either. It just sells the quality of the product.

The national ad, with repetitive messages about quality or safety, suggests that the next time you consider a car purchase you will consider Ford among your options. It gives you reasons "why," like safety or reliability. It *informs*, but doesn't really *entice.*

But what about the Ford dealer in your city? What should his message be? Should he spend his advertising dollars trying to sell the quality of the Ford product? No. He doesn't have enough money to do that. Ford Motor Company spends millions of dollars annually to do that. His $20,000 a month budget would be less than a drop in the great blue motion of a sunlit sea.

His ads should go after the people who are looking for a car today, and show them which cars he has and at what price. Hopefully, the national Ford ads did what they were supposed to do in convincing the marketplace that the Ford product is worth considering.

The local Ford dealer needs to *entice* customers into his location. And the people most likely to react have already been favorably predisposed to the Ford product.

Listen to local radio ads for car dealerships. You will be amazed at how many of them spend the entire length of the message trying to sell their image, or the image of the brand they sell.

"It's Sale Day at Fidgety Ford! At Fidgety Ford, we have all the new Fords…from the sporty Mustang to the classy Contour…from the rugged F-150 to the family fun of a new Explorer."

Well, you just mentioned the same product the other four Ford dealers in your town carry. What have you said that will make them come to you?

"At Fidgety Ford, we have the friendliest sales staff on the

planet! You can trust us to give you the lowest prices and best service in town."

Sure! A recent survey I read asked respondents to rank the most respected professions. Guess which profession ranked at the <u>bottom</u>? I don't know why, because I've known a lot of honorable, respectable car salesmen over the years. But our impression of the guy in the plaid jacket with the multi-colored tie, the baggy pants, slick hair and mustache and the big cigar looming from a sarcastic smile, came from somewhere.

The image is enhanced by the fact that automobile sales are negotiable. There are so many ways to hide profit, and the car salesman who excels will give you the illusion that you got a "good deal." In reality, you probably paid the same, or maybe even more, than you would have at any of the competitors.

"So let Fidgety Ford put you in the car you want at the price you can afford. We're the home of the great deals."

Rhetoric, rhetoric, rhetoric! This guy just wasted 30 seconds of airtime and the price of the spot.

All they're doing is helping other competitive car dealers sell the same product. What they *should* be doing is getting you to come to *their* location.

Remember that you can only do three things with your message . . .inform, entertain or entice. And you can combine these things. You can get some good information across in an entertaining fashion. You can entice someone to come to your furniture store by informing them about a sale. But you must have realistic expectations about the results. More about realistic expectations later.

You can't always expect an entertaining ad to entice someone. How many ads can you describe the story line for, but can't remember the brand name? Probably a great many of them.

It happens every Super Bowl Sunday. New spots are introduced by major sponsors, and people stand around the water cooler the next day to discuss how funny this one or that one was. But in most cases, they can't remember the name of the product advertised.

Before you can determine what you want to do with your message, we must discuss some of the basic rudiments of advertising. But first, let's distinguish between the big national advertiser and the small local advertiser.

"We grew up founding our dreams on the infinite promise of American advertising. I still believe that one can learn to play piano by mail and that mud will give you a perfect complexion."

Zelda Fitzgerald –

"Save Me A Waltz"

Chapter Six
Macro vs. Micro Advertisers

The best way for me to distinguish the national advertiser from the local advertiser is to call national advertisers *macro-advertisers.*

This icon of the industry constitutes about 45% of total advertising revenues. They are the Coca Colas and Microsofts, the Reeboks and the Bud Lights.

These are the companies that the average consumer talks about if the discussion turns to advertising. These are the campaigns that garner respect and awards in the industry, thereby opening doors to new *macro-advertisers* and huge budgets.

For the industry leaders advertising agencies were born. And to the top of the ranks of these ad agencies went the Harvard graduates… or the occasional creative mind in small markets around the country who created extremely successful campaigns. Small markets were their stepping stones. These were the best of the best.

Their gathering place became a stretch of road in Manhattan called Madison Avenue. It seemed natural, since the largest numbers of macro-advertisers were headquartered in New York. It sure cut down on travel time!

Madison Avenue became the top of the mountain, the standard

by which <u>all</u> advertising agencies were judged. On these streets walked J. Walter Thompson and David Ogilvey, the pioneers of modern advertising.

Madison Avenue became a very powerful influence on society. Their messages helped build huge industries and enhanced the images of giants. Every advertising executive in America aspires either to be on Madison Avenue, or create their own Madison Avenue in their community.

This is where the *macro-advertiser* wants to be, and they will spend whatever it takes to be there-- even if it doesn't work. Because if it doesn't, there's more than one big agency on Madison Avenue. Believe me, there are thousands of horror stories about expensive campaigns that garnered less than profitable results.

The *macro-advertisers* spend hundreds of thousands of dollars producing high quality ads. It always amazed me that agencies would hire expensive models, fly them and an entire crew, including make-up artists and two or three "assistant directors" to a remote island in the Caribbean, stay for a week or more in high priced hotels, all for the purpose of about 30 seconds of footage for a television commercial selling mascara. The client has to pay for all this. How much does mascara cost? About $4. Do you know how much mascara they would have to sell just to pay for the location shoot?!

Then they have to spend more to finish editing the spot. They've spent $300,000, and they haven't even put one commercial on the air yet. They have to sell 75,000 units of mascara <u>before</u> they go on the air just to pay for the production of the commercial!

What's even more amazing is that they wouldn't keep doing it if it didn't work. These big agencies do it all the time. And businesses keep putting up the money. It <u>must</u> work!

The *macro-advertisers* don't buy local news, they buy National news. They buy most of the prime-time spots, and spend billions on sports programming throughout the year.

These *macro-advertisers* hire the high profile advertising agencies. They come armed with credentials of glory. The finest art directors, the best researchers, the most creative copywriters. And fees big enough to pay for it all.

These are the giants. These are the *macro-advertisers*.

The Micro-Advertisers

But what about the businesses that have to advertise in order to compete in today's over-communicated society…the ones that don't have the large budgets available to them like the macro-advertisers do.

I call these the *micro-advertisers*. The *micro-advertiser* is the lifeblood of newspapers, radio stations and television stations. The *micro-advertiser* supports all the peripheral advertising venues in America…direct mail, neighborhood newspapers, the local specialty magazines and the cable stations.

These are the businesses that you <u>don't</u> hear people talk about on a day-to-day basis when the discussion turns to advertising.

"Did you see the new Budweiser ad in the Super Bowl? It was great!"

"Oh yeah, well you should have seen the new ad for Barney's Ford! It <u>really</u> moved me!"

I don't think so!

The *micro-advertiser* can't afford to spend hundreds of thousands of dollars on production of spots. They can't hire big talent. There are no travel budgets. They can't afford film production; they can only afford the lower quality videotape production. You know what it looks like. You can usually tell a local commercial from a national commercial just by the quality…or lack of quality.

They can't afford to buy prime time ads, and can barely afford radio's drive time.

And they don't need expensive advertising agencies to create their campaigns. They need every dime just to get their message in front of the consumer.

They don't need creative awards. They need results!

These are the *micro-advertisers.* They constitute 55% of all the money spent on advertising in America. That's a <u>lot</u> of money! Over a billion dollars a year.

This book is written for the benefit of the *micro-advertiser.* And for the people who buy the advertising, the people who sell the advertising, the ones who create the advertising and the people who are the recipients of the messages. That would be just about everyone!

It is written for all the businesses out there that have ever lost money on advertising. That would include most of them.

I recently taught a seminar for a group of national business owners. There were about 300 people in the audience. I asked, by a show of hands, how many had ever lost money on advertising. About 300 hands raised. It fits in nicely with my theory that most advertising is either ineffective or not as effective as it could be.

What numeric figure becomes the parameter between the macro-advertiser and the micro-advertiser? It is different in every market.

Based on advertising rates in New York City, and considering the population base there, a micro-advertiser could have a budget of up to $1,000,000 a month.

In any other major market, the maximum budget for a micro-advertiser could be up to $500,000 a month. And in most small markets, they could spend as much as $50,000 a month.

A good distinction could be made in the car business. A Toyota dealer moving up to 500 cars a month in some major markets could spend $200,000 a month or more on local advertising. But the regional Toyota Dealer Group, which constitutes <u>all</u> the Toyota dealers in a designated area, has a lot more money to spend than the local dealer does. And Toyota Motor Company has even more to spend on a national buy.

But that's the car business. There are hundreds of other businesses out there in middle America that don't have the kind of profit margin car dealers have, but they <u>still</u> need the business. And they <u>still</u> have competitors, maybe a lot more. They need to advertise. They are easy targets to fall into the category of the 65% of all businesses that will fold within five years.

The macro-advertisers have unlimited financial resources to create their campaigns. The micro-advertisers do not.

The macro-advertisers need help. That's why they have Madison Avenue. The micro-advertisers usually can't afford help or don't think they need help. But in most cases, they do.

People are unhappy (and neurotic) in America today because advertising has caused them to have unrealistic expectations of life, themselves, their jobs and the Fantasyland products and services that are constantly pushed on them.

--Curtis Smale

Kirk Donovan

Chapter Seven
Realistic Expectations

John Wannemaker, founder of the famous old New York Department store bearing his name and one of the country's first major micro-advertisers, once said, "Only half of all advertising works. I only wish I knew <u>which</u> half!"

He knew what he was talking about. He was probably the single largest advertiser in the country at the time. And he said <u>that</u> in 1907! That's even before we <u>became</u> the over-communicated society.

If only half of all advertising worked back then, imagine what the percentage is today! More reinforcement for my theory that 85% of all advertising is either ineffective or not as effective as it could be.

It was a lot easier back then. When Wannemaker's ad said a product was the "best," people believed it. They had no other frame of reference. Society didn't have nearly the amount of competition-per-brand in <u>any</u> category.

Before mass communication created mass competition, people pretty much knew what they needed and where to get it.

Department stores were created for convenience. More "things" in one place than ever before. As society grew, the need for convenience grew. As technology grew, industries were born. As industries became enormously successful, mass communication chronicled those successes and painted possibilities for a restless America. And it redefined *business success.*

As America grew, and industry prospered, Darwin's theories became more apparent. *Survival of the fittest* transcended from the human species to corporate America.

Consumers, and the money they controlled, were influenced by mass communication to abandon Mom and Pop's businesses. They had to retire.

Today's independent businessman grew up watching the rise of corporate America. All he wanted was his piece of the pie.

And the dichotomy between the macro-advertiser and the micro-advertiser began to take shape.

The macro-advertiser spends millions of dollars creating images, which is <u>very</u> important. How could I sell a Ford Taurus at an incredible price if Ford Motor Company hadn't done *it's* job developing the credibility of the Ford product?

And the macro-advertiser <u>can</u> wait to see the results. They know it takes a lot of time and a lot of money to move America.

But the micro-advertiser can't wait. He doesn't have the money to wait. He needs it to work <u>now</u>. And he expects it to work now. He can't move America. He only needs to move a small fraction of it.

Probably the most difficult job I had representing micro-advertisers over the years was helping them determine *realistic expectations.*

When it came to the micro-advertiser, expectations usually exceeded possibilities. And the smaller the advertiser, the greater the expectations.

They probably know that 65% of all businesses fail, and they won't accept failure. When business is down, they'll try whatever it takes to build it back up. But their patience, like their money, runs thin.

So here I come, selling them a schedule on my radio station.

"It didn't work!" I would hear.

"Well, it's your first time on the air. It takes a while to build your reputation."

What I'm actually saying is "You need to spend more money." That's easy for me to say. It's not <u>my</u> money. And it's very difficult for him to hear because it <u>is</u> <u>his</u> money!

To advertise effectively, you have to develop realistic expectations.

There are basically two ways to spend your advertising dollars with *potential* effectiveness. Now, keep in mind there are many elements to a successful campaign, like the message and the media selected. But there are still two ways to spend your money effectively.

You can spend a <u>lot</u> of money over a relatively short time span. This type of advertising is used for retail sales events, introduction of new products, grand openings, etc.

Or, you can spend a <u>little</u> money over a relatively long time span. This is image advertising, or *institutional* advertising.

But don't expect to spend a <u>small</u> amount of money over a <u>short</u> time span and get the kind of results the other two methods produce.

If it could be done that way, the other guys would probably catch on and quit spending the large amounts of money! That is the reality of the beast.

So, how do you determine realistic expectations? Unfortunately, there are no easy answers. Every business is different. I make my living analyzing businesses to help determine what those expectations should be, and every business is different.

First, you must determine if you want your advertising to entertain, inform or entice.

With institutional advertising, or advertising which tries to create, maintain or reinforce an "image," you should expect a long-term commitment.

Let's say you're introducing a new soap powder to a marketplace inundated with soap powders. We'll call our product "Kudzu Cleaner."

Now, if you're walking down the soap aisle at the grocery store and you see *Tide, Cheer, Clorox* and Kudzu, which would you probably <u>not</u> choose? Kudzu, of course. You've never heard of it before. And you <u>have</u> heard about the others your entire life.

There are some Americans who scamper to try <u>anything</u> new, but the percentage is slim. A survey of grocery store managers shows that generic products account for only 4% of sales.

Generic products have no name recognition within the public's mind, just like new, never-before-introduced products.

We have to create an image, over a long period of time, chipping away at the buying habits soap-buyers have had for years.

And don't think you can do it with words like "new" or "better," because the established products say those things all the time, too.

Before Kudzu Cleaner can become a household name, it has to become a recognized name. And that takes time. And a lot of money.

I heard throughout my academic career that research shows the average person needs to hear something seven times before they remember it.

That research was done before we became the over-communicated society. Now we're deluged with messages and products and promises. That *Rule of Seven* can't possibly be accurate any more. With all the clutter, you may have to hear something over 14 times before it begins to sink in.

It takes a constant barrage of information over a long period of time for a product to become credible. This is especially true for the macro-advertiser. The micro-advertiser doesn't have a long period of time. Their message usually needs to entice an action to occur immediately, or within a short period of time.

DONOVAN'S FISHING ANALOGY

Let's go fishing for customers. After all, advertising, in general, is a lot like fishing.

Our job with advertising is to go out and find as many people as we can who will take our "bait."

There are essentially four elements to being a good fisherman. First is the number of lines you have in the water. The fisherman with the most lines in the water potentially will catch the most fish. This becomes an element of how many ads you have the ability, or budget, to buy.

When we run an advertisement in the newspaper, we find one place and leave our line in the water all day … in the same place.

The next element is to know exactly where the fish are.

Let's say we're advertising for a Greek restaurant. We need to find as many hungry people as we possibly can. So, let's run a newspaper ad in the restaurant section.

Now, if you are a good fisherman, you <u>know</u> the key to success is to go where the most fish are. That's common sense.

Newspaper advertising is excellent for targeting big schools of fish in one place each day. This is especially true of products that reach specifically targeted audiences.

For instance, if we're trying to do recruitment advertising for a local business college, we know there's a lot of "fish" around the

Schools section of the classifieds. And most important, they're hungry for <u>our</u> type of bait.

If our "fish" are looking for discounts on grocery products, we have a favorite spot for them...once or twice a week, every week, in just about every newspaper in America.

The third element in the fishing analogy is understanding that the fish move. They usually don't stay in one spot. If we find a fishing spot that works one morning, it won't work every morning. The fish catch on. When the sun moves, they move to warmer waters. They have the entire Continental Shelf as their "stompin' ground." They may, however, by being creatures of habit, go back to the same place at certain times. The skill is <u>knowing</u> those times.

The public also moves around in their advertising consumption habits. If you run the same ad over and over, directed at the same audience, the message becomes redundant and rhetorical, and unfortunately, resilient.

With newspaper advertising, your school of fish on any given day is determined by the circulation of that newspaper. On radio, it's the number of people listening at any given time. With television it's the number of people viewing any given program on a particular station at a particular time.

The final element to potentially catching the most fish is having the proper bait. If you're fishing in the Pacific Ocean, with more lines in the water than anyone else, exactly where the fish are, you won't catch any if you are using worms. Saltwater fish don't eat worms. The bait is the <u>message</u>. You need the proper hook and bait to attract the fish you want to catch.

I sold advertising to a gentleman one day who insisted that my station didn't reach his audience. After much persistence, he relented. He gave me a small budget one weekend to try it out.

He created the message, a rhetorical, institutional theme with no real reason to shop his store <u>today</u>. On Monday morning, I went back to see him.

"I told you it wouldn't work!" he said. So I told him that if he would try one more time, I would give him a free 60 second spot on Friday afternoon during the peak afternoon-drive hours.

"You can say whatever you want for the first 50 seconds" I said, "but in the last 10 seconds of the ad, we would announce that the first 50 people who showed up at his door on Saturday morning would get a free $100 bill."

"Are you ready to try it?" I asked.

Well of course he wasn't. If I <u>did</u> have listeners, he would have to cough up $5000.

"But it doesn't matter," I said. "If no one is listening to my station, you won't get anyone to respond anyway."

The bait the message has to be attractive to the fish or they won't nibble.

It's rather disconcerting to think of people as fish. Especially since I'm a person, and a consumer who is influenced by advertising. But the analogy can't be much clearer. If we learn to become good fishermen, our chances of catching more fish increase.

Quality, value, style, service, selection, convenience, economy, savings, performance, experience, hospitality, low rates, friendly service, name brands, easy terms, affordable prices, money back guarantee, free installation.

Free admission, free appraisal, free alterations, free delivery, free estimates, free home trial, free parking.

No cash, no problem. No muss, no fuss, no risk, no obligation, no red tape, no down payment, no entry fee, no hidden charges, no purchase necessary, no one will call you, no payment or interest till September.

Limited time only, act now, order today, send no money, offer good while supplies last, each item sold separately, batteries not included, mileage may vary, all sales final, allow 6 weeks for delivery, some items not available, some assembly required, some restrictions may apply.

Come on in for a free demonstration and free consultation with our friendly, professional staff. Our experienced and knowledgeable sales representatives will help you make a selection that's just right for you and just right for your budget.

Pick up your free gift...a classic, deluxe, custom designer, luxury, prestigious, high quality, premium, select gourmet pocket pencil sharpener. Yours for the asking. No purchase necessary. It's our way of saying thank you.

And if you act right now, we'll include an extra added free complimentary bonus gift...a genuine imitation leather style carrying case with authentic vinyl trim!

George Carlin monologue

Chapter Eight
The Rhetoric of Advertising

It's enough to make you dizzy! But these are words and phrases you hear every day. You probably heard a lot of them today! You become so immune to them that they fly by you when you hear them. Such is the nature of the rhetoric of advertising.

Our minds and imaginations are plummeted with over 1500 messages each day. That's over 60 messages throughout each waking hour. A message a minute since the day you were born! That's a lot of impressions.

The messages hit us in the form of print ads, radio and television ads, billboards. Every logo you see on a shirt, or shoes, or on the back of an automobile is an impression.

Success for major products and services has come to the ones who could spend the most money and create messages that stick. And even that isn't enough for most, because other well-financed competitors outspend and outwit the giants, chipping away at their dominant shares of the marketplace.

The most recognizable names suddenly had to become "new" and "improved." In most cases, it was the same product as before. The only thing that changed was the packaging and the advertising.

In our language, there are an abundance of adjectives. But in the big scheme of things, there are only <u>so</u> many adjectives. So advertisers have abused the privilege of the rhetoric available to them. We're so immersed in "bigger and better" that the effect of the words have become resilient.

These adjectives have been thrown around for dozens of years. It's like the word "love." When someone says "I love you" every hour of every day, it loses some of it's impact.

Another analogy is using the word *free*. Everyone knows that <u>nothing</u> is free! In most cases, the cost of the item is built somewhere into the price.

Take the word "quality." How many times have you heard that label for a product, only to find out that there are other similar products with <u>better</u> quality for your taste?

Or the word "affordable." Who is the advertised item affordable to? A new Lexus might be affordable to you, but is it affordable to everyone?

Another misused term is "friendly."

"Visit our friendly staff today and see what we can do for you."

I recently went to a restaurant that stated they had the friendliest people in town. I didn't receive one smile. There was very little eye contact. When my bill was presented, there was no *thank you for your business.* No one taught these people the importance of nonverbal communication in friendliness. They were just taught to say *please* and *thank you,* verbal expressions of politeness, but not how to say it with expressiveness. Very few businesses today teach nonverbal communication.

Another example of the rhetoric of advertising is in the word "taste."

"We have the best food in town" or "The best tasting Italian food you've ever eaten."

Doesn't everyone have different determinations of what tastes good to them? What if I told you that I was serving the best liver in town? Do you like liver? How can I be so pretentious to think that everyone likes liver, much less the <u>best</u> liver?!

Haven't you been lured by advertising that says "the best" food in town, only to be revolted by steak that is too thin or cooked too well, or vegetables that are soggy? It's happened to all of us, I'm sure.

So what do we believe anymore? Does the rhetoric of advertising still work in our over-communicated society?

How can an automobile ad claim that a new Honda Civic is

the perfect car for you? Maybe you don't like Hondas. Maybe you'd rather drive a Mercedes. All right, then drive a new Mercedes…the perfect car for you. What if you can't afford a Mercedes? It <u>isn't</u> the perfect car for you!

How many times do you hear that a business is "conveniently" located? If you live on the south side of town and hear that a business on the north side of town is convenient to you, do you wonder who the message is addressing itself to? *Convenience* is different to each person. Yet you hear the word all the time.

With over 1000 messages a day, we're bombarded with the best, the biggest, the tastiest, the friendliest, the new and improved, the most advanced, the least expensive, the most expensive, the most convenient…do these people really think we're that stupid!

So these commonly used advertising words become redundant and rhetorical, which eventually makes them resilient. We ignore what we hear because we've all been burned before.

I'm not sure there's a single adjective that has not been overused in the world of advertising rhetoric. Should we take these words out of our advertising vocabulary? It would be impossible.

What we must do is limit our <u>expectations</u> of the results when we rely only on rhetoric. Don't rely on the public responding to these words alone. The landscape of failed businesses is littered with misused adjectives that didn't work. The public has caught on.

Kirk Donovan

And like a good neighbor,
State Farm is there.

Kirk Donovan

Chapter Nine
Positioning

Before being able to determine which response you want to elicit from your advertising message, there are other behavioral science techniques you should understand. One of the most important techniques is to *position* your product.

Al Ries and Jack Trout, in their landmark book *"Positioning,"* describe positioning as <u>not</u> what you do with your product, but what you do to the *mind* of your prospect. The basic approach is to manipulate information that is already in the mind, to "retie the connections that already exist."

The book was published in the early 1980s, when the world seemed like it could bear very little more marketing communication. Positioning was a good start on the road to breaking through the clutter. But since then, the computer revolution and increased media options have added even <u>more</u> to the clutter.

Positioning, as an advertising theory, introduced a new way of creating and analyzing the message. For the first time, copywriters began using a psychological approach in an attempt to achieve results. The rhetoric of advertising had become so over-saturated that the public started to catch on.

We needed new ways to devise "sneak attacks" on the mind

of the wary consumer. With more and more products available to the marketplace, we had to find ways to *position* our product away from the others, or in some cases, closer to the competition.

What that means is that some businesses realize they don't have enough money to surpass the #1 competitor in their field. But they can certainly cut deep into #3's share of the market. That becomes their ultimate goal.

Just saying "new and improved" or "we're the biggest" didn't work as effectively anymore, because no one believed it. The message became rhetorical and resilient.

The Un-Cola Wars

A perfect example of positioning was the campaign by the #3 selling soft drink brand in the country. Clearly dominating the soft drink industry were the two Cola giants, Pepsi Cola and Coca-Cola. 7-Up knew that the only chance of getting the kind of market share of Coke or Pepsi was to spend a <u>lot</u> of money.

The other two companies had spent enough money in advertising over the years to solidify their dominance, so even with 7-Up outspending both of them; it would still be unlikely they would catch up with them. It would take too many years of outspending them. So 7-Up, through a combination of realistic expectations and positioning, created a new campaign.

By determining realistic expectations, 7-Up decided their goal would not be to match Coke or Pepsi in sales, but to climb above the clutter of all the <u>other</u> soft drinks on the market. A much easier goal to reach!

Next came the positioning of their product away from the other competitors and toward Coke and Pepsi. Coca-Cola spent millions of dollars each year advertising two words . . .*Coca* and *Cola*. Pepsi Cola spent millions of dollars a year advertising two words...*Pepsi* and *Cola*.

The one common word that benefits from the combined millions is *Cola.* 7-Up decided to offer an alternative to all those people who did not like Colas, so they smartly became the "<u>Un</u>-Cola." They positioned themselves above the pack and became the #3 selling soft drink brand.

Another famous example of positioning was the campaign launched by the Avis Rental Car Company. Well behind industry leader Hertz in annual revenues, Avis positioned themselves with all the people out there who favor the underdog. "We're #2" they claimed. And "We try harder." The self-fulfilling prophecy led them to become #2.

In advertising, positioning strategy should not be overlooked. If you want to win the customer, you must understand the reasons <u>why</u> they desire your product. You must get on their wavelength. And being the first is not always enough. As Ries and Trout point out, IBM didn't invent the computer. It was Sperry Rand. IBM, however, was the first to <u>position</u> the computer in the mind of the public. Sperry Rand no longer exists.

Part of the reason for the failure of most advertising is the inability to position the product in the consumers' mind. Ries and Trout's book focused on national advertising campaigns that found success through positioning. But can it be done by the small advertiser? If you are creative, yes it <u>can</u> be done.

For many years, I consulted for one of the country's oldest and most respected Ford dealers, Beaudry Ford in downtown Atlanta. The dealership had been selling Fords in Atlanta since 1916.

Throughout the years, as the suburbs grew, all the car dealers moved out of downtown and into suburbia. Beaudry Ford was the only one left. It became more and more difficult to get prospective buyers to drive downtown. We decided to position the dealership in three ways.

First, the fact that they were in Atlanta so long was a positive, because they established themselves with many of Georgia's largest corporations as a supplier of fleets of vehicles. I used that in my endeavors to reach the retail Ford customer. Because Beaudry sold so many vehicles, one positioning strategy was to convince potential customers that volume selling meant savings to them as individuals.

Trustworthiness and reputation were the focus of the second

positioning strategy. How could a car dealer be around since 1916 if they weren't dependable?

The final strategy became their central location. A huge percentage of car buyers still comparison shop. By being in the direct center of the population, it made sense to tell shoppers to use Beaudry as their comparison since it was the next closest dealer to them.

These three positioning strategies kept Beaudry Ford competitive in Atlanta for many years, helping to overcome the tremendous disadvantage of being downtown.

The Waterbed Dilemma

Another example of local positioning was done for a small waterbed store in the suburbs of Atlanta. My client was located near a new shopping mall, at least 10 miles from "waterbed row."

This was in the late 1980s, when the industry was peaking. Waterbed stores spent thousands of dollars on radio stations every weekend promoting various sales events. There was a "waterbed war" going on.

On an access road along a major interstate were 6 stores that continuously participated in the waterbed wars. Each of the stores on waterbed row averaged spending about $20,000 a month on radio each month. That's $120,000 a month in ads telling people to come to that street if they wanted to buy a waterbed. Different messages, different music, different prices, but all with a common message…waterbeds are for sale on this street.

A few exits away on the interstate was Waterbed Showcase, my client. He was new, and only had $3000 a month to spend on advertising, certainly a lot less than the established waterbed stores.

The positioning strategy was simple…there is another choice. But how could we stand out amongst all the competitors that were outspending us? I procured a billboard right in the middle of waterbed row. In huge letters it read

"WATERBED?

You're on the wrong street!
Waterbed Showcase, 2 exits north."

The message was very concise, not too wordy, and quite effective.

The combined advertising dollars of all those other waterbed stores were to get people in the market for a waterbed to come to that street. Our message simply offered another choice on another street. The billboard was the most effective advertising that Waterbed Showcase ever did. And it was the least expensive.

These examples of positioning strategy prove a very important advertising edict. To be successful in business, you do <u>not</u> necessarily have to outspend the competition. You can win by outthinking them. But you can't hope to be successful in any advertising effort if you don't consider how you want to position your product or service in the mind of the consumer.

You must also determine how you want to position your business realistically amongst your competitors. That, too, is done in the mind of the consumer. If you are number one in your category, you must position yourself to *stay* there. If you are number four, you must first get to number three. Then number two. And when you're number two, you must continually look back at number three, because they're probably coming after you!

In today's over-communicated society, the battle is for the mind of the consumer. Business is war. Consider some of the most often used advertising terms: a campaign, a strategy, a sales blitz. This is the rhetoric of war. It can be done with taste and class. It can be done with daggers. That is determined by individual business philosophies. But whatever tactic is used, it is still a battle for the mind of the consumer.

Earlier I mentioned the huge number of business failures each year. The businesses that succeed are run by generals who understand the necessity to compete and the complexities required for doing so. Positioning is essential in determining the ground rules for competition.

Advertising is, actually, a simple phenomenon in terms of economics. It is merely a substitute for a personal sales force--an extention of the merchant who cries aloud his wares.

--Rosser Reeves

Kirk Donovan

Chapter Ten
AdSense

Stanley Redd has been a loyal friend and business partner over the years. He's often been heard to say that I had a "unique ability to point out the obvious." That _is_ AdSense.

Stanley was at a seminar I conducted. A woman described her dilemma. She was running radio ads requesting that people pick up the phone and call her to order her product.

"I'm not getting many phone calls," she said. "I've spent a lot of money on radio. What can I do?"

"Don't buy radio," I responded rapidly and succinctly. "Try television. The phone is usually within walking distance of the TV. So if someone is interested, they will pick up the phone and call you. If they are driving somewhere in their car and become interested in your product, you are relying on them to remember your phone number once they get to a phone. They would probably have to hear your ad numerous times before they were able to respond. With television, all they have to do is reach for the phone."

"_I_ could have thought of _that_!" she playfully acknowledged. But she didn't. Never overlook the obvious. _That_ is AdSense.

Today's advertising business is built around statistical science.

It is bought and sold based on statistical science.

But, as I described earlier, the ultimate purpose of advertising is to get a response. The future of advertising for the "micro-advertiser" will have to utilize the *behavioral* science of advertising, or **AdSense.**

I want you to participate in an exercise with me. The purpose will be to show you that advertising messages require <u>more</u> than just creativity.

One of the principle ingredients of AdSense is salience. The dictionary describes salience as "strikingly conspicuous, or pertaining to." I will redefine salience by example. I'll create a scene for you, so follow along with me.

We're sitting in my office talking. It doesn't matter what we're talking about. You can insert your own verbal scenario. In my office is a big picture window, through which is seen the parking lot to a small restaurant. Again, follow along.

We're both dressed in nice, expensive business clothes, it's pouring down rain outside, and there is no umbrella in the room. I glance out the window and say, "Wow! It's pouring down rain out there!"

Now, you <u>heard</u> me. You received an auditory signal. You respond nonverbally by glancing toward the window. And you may verbally respond, "It sure is." Then we continue our previous conversation.

I'll now show you the impact of <u>salience</u> by adding just one element to our scene. We're getting ready to walk across that parking lot to the restaurant for lunch. I say, "Wow! It's pouring down rain out there!"

By adding that one element, the same statement you heard earlier, the one you responded to both verbally and nonverbally, suddenly became salient. It will create or change a physical behavioral response. In this case, we won't walk out the door yet. Or we'll get wet!

Salience, in AdSense terminology, is something that will change, alter or create a <u>behavioral</u> response. In our scene, it would <u>change</u> a behavioral response. We were getting ready to walk out the door into a rainstorm with no umbrella. Now, we'll wait. We postponed our response.

In all the years I've been involved in the advertising business, through all the advertising "experts" I've encountered and advertising agencies I've heard pitch their plans, no one has <u>ever</u> talked about salience. They talked about creative awards and cost-per-point. But not salience. That is unfortunate, because it is <u>the</u> most important element of AdSense.

To be successful in advertising, you <u>must</u> understand your target audience. Then, you must analyze what it is about your product or service that is salient to that audience. That's done with a combination of statistical science and behavioral science, not just the traditional statistical way.

Deeper Into Salience

Here are some other examples of using salience in your thought process, based on experiences I've had throughout my career.

There was an automobile dealer called Dodge Country In the northern suburbs of Atlanta. The owner, Bill Newton, is a long-time client and friend. When I began consulting with Bill on his advertising, I made some bold suggestions. My advice went against the grain of the traditional car dealer advertising.

Over the years, the main advertising medium used by car dealers has been the newspaper classifieds. As a society, we've been trained that when we want to look for a car, we go to the local newspapers classified automobile section.

We're also conditioned to go to the theater section to find out what time our movie starts and where to go. We're conditioned to go to the newspaper on certain days to get our grocery coupons.

We're conditioned to go to the newspaper to look for job interviews. And we've been conditioned to go to the newspaper to look for deals on cars. Newspaper revenues dominate all other media combined when it comes to automobile advertising.

The reason most of these *conditionings* are related to newspaper advertising is that newspapers have been selling ads much longer than other traditional media. Television and radio have been advertising forces for less than a century. Benjamin Franklin sold ads in Poor Richard's Almanac in 1733. Newspaper advertising had quite a head start.

My suggestion for Dodge Country was to get out of the newspaper. Try television advertising. Bill looked at me with shock and amazement.

"O.K." he said. "Justify your suggestion."

There were several reasons for my recommendation. One goes back a long way.

As a young teenager in Southern California, I used to sit and watch television every Saturday morning. It was the mid-1960s, and Ralph Williams had discovered television advertising. Ralph Williams Ford ran 30-second commercials in what seemed like every break. He would pitch primarily used cars, and the spots were done live, so each spot was different.

In one, he would be standing next to a beat up looking car

with a big $999 painted on the windshield. There stood this big, gruff sounding guy in a cheap suit yelling about how great a deal it was. Then he would pick up a big sledgehammer and smash the windshield!

"$699!" he would yell!

In the next spot, he would have a dog sitting on the hood of another car. He would be talking to the dog about how great a deal this was. I used to laugh like crazy. But I remembered Ralph Williams Ford. And guess where I bought my first car? I always <u>knew</u> that television must be a good medium for selling vehicles.

There was another reason. Just down the street from Dodge Country was the highest-volume car dealer in Atlanta, a dealer that spent over three times more on advertising than the next leading car advertiser. This dealership budgeted over $150,000 a month on Atlanta television and continuously sold over 500 vehicles a month. They did it with no newspaper or radio… just television.

Now, remember positioning? This dealership down the street spent all that money each month telling people who were looking for a car to get off at <u>their</u> exit on the interstate. Every single ad was different. Different sales events, different prices. But <u>every</u> message had one thing in common. If you're looking for a car, get off at this exit.

Well, we couldn't spend even a third of that guy's budget, but we did have one really important thing in common with that them. <u>We</u> were off their exit!

The Analysis

Next, I analyzed a statistical consideration. Remember, I said AdSense is a blend of statistical and behavioral science. On any given day, anywhere in the United States, only about 1% of the population is in the market for a car. That percentage can vary slightly, according to economic conditions, climatic condition, and many other variables. But for the most part, on any given day, only 1% of the driving population is a legitimate prospect. We're talking about a new or used car, truck, van or anything.

Being in the market for a car doesn't necessarily mean you're looking <u>today</u>. Your lease may be expiring in two months. You may be having more and more problems with your current car. You may have gotten a raise and can soon afford a better car. Your kid may be getting his license and you're beginning to explore. <u>That</u> is being in the 1% in the market for a car. It doesn't mean that 1% of the population will actually be driving around looking for a car or making a purchase today.

So who is the salient audience for a car dealer on any given day? It's that 1% who <u>are</u> in the market for a car <u>today</u>.

As a car dealer trying to find ways of reaching that salient audience, there's another statistic that makes it even <u>more</u> agonizing. What percentage of that car buying population is in the market for <u>their</u> line of cars? Out of all the cars sold in this country, the Dodge line of cars and trucks captures about 7%. So on any given day, only 7% of 1% are potentially in the market for one of these vehicles. That is Dodge Country's salient audience <u>today</u>.

So <u>why</u> not recommend newspaper advertising for Dodge Country? First, let's look at it from a "statistical" perspective. Newspaper rates are based on circulation. The prices you pay are statistically derived. The newspaper reaches a certain amount of people every day through circulation. Based on the number of those subscribers, a price for an ad can be established and justified by a low cost-per-thousand.

But as behavioral scientists, we must add to the cost factor a <u>very</u> important element. On any given day, only about 1% of the people getting the newspaper will open the classified automobile section! When you buy an ad in that classified section, you are paying for everyone getting the newspaper that day. But only 1% will put themselves in a position to read that ad, unless, maybe, it is on the back page. And wait till you see how expensive <u>that</u> is!

Even then, if they're not in the market for a car, chances are likely they will not respond to your message. If they're not looking for a car, the ad isn't salient. Even if they see a great price on a car but don't need it, they won't respond. No offense. They just don't need a car right now.

There are two things you can do with your advertising message. You can get people to *note* your message. The more "notations," the better chance the audience has of remembering you once your product becomes salient to them.

The other thing, of course, is to get them to *respond* to your message. The ones with the potential to respond are your <u>salient</u> audience, or the ones in the market for a car.

I told Bill that if I bought a television ad on the 6 o'clock news, the same premise would hold true for television as it did for newspaper. Only 1% of the viewers are in the market for a car. But the rest have an opportunity to note the ad. In the newspaper, they have to turn to that section. And who would spend time in the classified auto section of the newspaper if they aren't looking for a car? Why would they if they are not in the market for a car? No exposure...no notation.

On television, you've <u>got</u> them. And you can show them the actual vehicle in motion, not a line drawing or a hardly-visible picture like you get with newsprint.

Salience of the Medium

Well, I had provided enough information for Dodge Country to try television advertising. But the process of AdSense didn't stop once we determined which media we were going to use. Salience is as important to the <u>message</u> as it is to the <u>medium</u>. Here is the thought process used in the case of Dodge Country's creative effort.

The Dodge product line is targeted to Middle America. Middle America is the mainstay of our economy. It is the vast expanse of humanity who live from paycheck to paycheck with a little left over for savings and retirement. Because Middle America accounts for so much of our economy, most advertising is targeted to them.

Our over-communicated society inundates Middle America with a barrage of ways to dispose of what little disposable income is left over at the end of each month.

First let's detemine what is important to middle America when it comes to purchasing a car? What is the most salient point?

Over many years of consulting car dealers of all kinds, I've read dozens of customer satisfaction surveys. There were always questions asking for reasons behind their car purchase. There were many reasons.

Brand loyalty is important, but not as important as it used to be. There are so many choices now. And so many cars look alike.

Safety is very important, and reputation for dependability and quality. And of course, style is important. But there's one thing that surpasses all those other reasons in determining Middle America's choice for a new car.

Price? You're close. But let's say we advertised a new car for $23,575. Can Middle America determine what the monthly payment is when you finance $23,575? And can they do it in the time it takes them to see a 30 second television ad? Not many can.

The most important factor for middle-Americans in their decision making process is the <u>monthly payment</u>. How much income do I have to spend on a car payment each month? <u>That</u> is the salient point.

Will you respond to a message that gets your attention, even if you can't afford the product? You may see an ad for a new Jaguar that is absolutely gorgeous. It's the car you have always wanted. But if the payment is $800 a month and you can only afford $300 a month, you won't respond.

By using television ads showing several "sale" vehicles with attractive monthly payments, Dodge Country became one of the top selling Dodge dealers in Georgia. It was done without using the traditional newspaper advertising. And it was done while spending the same amount on advertising that was spent before we started doing television. We sold more than 100 cars more a month. Those advertising dollars were just spent more effectively.

By using salience to determine which media we must use to reach our potential audience, and using salience in creating a message that could entice that potential audience to react, we maximized the return on our investment.

This example isn't meant to attack the effectiveness of newspaper advertising for car dealers. I've dealt with some dealers who were very successful with their print ads. But with continuously rising prices in newspaper advertising costs, it's getting more and more difficult to be cost effective.

Do you see how important it is to consider the behavioral science of advertising? That is AdSense. Here are some more examples of how it works.

I consulted for the owner of an Italian restaurant. That's a tough job in a major city where Italian restaurants are plentiful. I asked him the purpose for his advertising. What was the response he wanted to elicit? He gave the generic answer. "To get more business," he said.

I hear that all the time, and it needs to be dissected. First, let's consider realistic expectations. Who is the most likely person to come to his restaurant? Someone who is hungry. That's a good start.

Next would be someone who is hungry for Italian food. Then, they need to be within driving distance of your restaurant. What can we possibly say to lure this, our salient audience, to your restaurant?

"We have great food?"

First of all, no one will believe it. Remember that we're bombarded with well over 1,000 messages each day! And how many times have we been promised things in advertising that weren't delivered? So, even if you <u>do</u> have the best food in town, no one will believe it when you tell them.

Secondly, let's say you <u>did</u> find someone who was hungry for Italian food. From where that person is when he sees or hears your message, how many Italian restaurants does he have to pass to get to <u>yours</u>? There could be dozens. Would you drive 20 miles, past ten or twelve Italian restaurants, to go to one that you heard about on the radio? One that claims they have the best Italian food in town? Possibly, but not likely. Remember, we've all been burned before!

So my challenge was to find a way to make this restaurant stand out from all the other Italian restaurants. What could I say about this restaurant that no other restaurant could say? Well, in this case, the restaurant <u>did</u> have something different. The building was attached to an old railroad dining car, and it sat right next to an old-but-still-used railroad track. I built my campaign around that as the salient point.

"Imagine," the copy said, "sitting in a little tratorria on a hillside near Rome. The music of Italy fills the room." Cue the music. "A train streaks past your window." Cue sound effect of train. "You're enjoying the flavors of classic Italy...well, you don't have far to go..."

Italian dining can be romantic. And there's also something romantic about a passing train. Put these together and you get a unique combination.

The copy, along with the good music and special sound effects, created a great radio commercial. And it was extremely successful. People <u>would</u> drive many miles, past dozens of Italian restaurants, to dine at this one because it was unique. And people respond to uniqueness.

Here's one more example of the impact of salience in creating advertising messages. The owner of a drug abuse clinic called me one day. He'd been running television ads soliciting patients. It was a very worthy company, but they weren't getting enough patients from the television ads to continue the expense.

I looked at their commercials. They were expensive, well-produced spots showing a guy who had just come out of rehabilitation. He stood there, with his wife and small daughter sitting next to him, thanking the company for saving his life and bringing his family back. It was very touching, with heart tugging music. It was one of those emotion-appealing ads that strike a cord in most people. But it didn't work.

So I started using a little AdSense. Who *is* the salient audience? It is someone who is addicted to drugs or alcohol. How can we define that audience? It's very difficult.

Addictive people come in many packages…different ages, many races, and in both sexes. There are rich addictive people and poor addictive people. Some are homeless; some have a wife and three kids in high school. They're all entirely different. So what <u>do</u> they have in common, other than their addiction? Ask a psychologist. They will tell you. The one salient commonality is <u>denial.</u>

The reason it's not easy to quit an addiction is that the person <u>denies</u> he or she has a problem. It's the common element of alcoholics. It's the common element of drug abusers. Otherwise, if they knew the dangers, they would probably quit. Look at all the evidence over the years that cigarette smoking can affect your health. Then look at all the smokers. Cancer won't strike me…that's denial.

So if I'm addressing an drug addict with a message that suggests "I can help break your drug addiction," they won't respond if they don't think they're addicted. And alcoholics don't think they're addicted.

To be effective, something has to be done to break through that denial. If you can't do that, you're spinning your wheels and wasting your money on sweet, emotional messages. You may even win a few creative awards. But you won't get patients.

My messages focused on the denial. One message was a close-up shot of a guy appearing to be sitting on the edge of a bed in a drab room. He looked like he had a really bad night, as he sat there in his dirty pajamas. He was looking right into the camera.

"I'm O.K., man, I just had a late night...a rough night. But I'll be O.K." Pause. "What's that? Drugs? Well, yeah, I did some. But I'm O.K. I know when to quit. My wife? Well, she left...but...she'll be back, man. She knows I'll quit."

He's getting angry with you, the one on the other end of the television screen, the one who's asking too many questions.

"Hey, I don't need to tell you <u>anything</u> man," he shouts! "I'm going to bed!"

The camera zooms out, revealing the man lying in an open coffin. As he lay back, he slams the coffin shut. On the screen are the words...

"You may be closer than you think!"

Sound a little over-dramatic? Well, maybe for you. You're not addicted. But to reach through denial, you have to get personal. And you have to be shocking.

It worked. The campaign focused entirely on denial and its consequences, and ended with a gentle suggestion that my client's organization was there to help. That organization helped a <u>lot</u> of people.

Salience has an enormous impact on any advertising campaign. This new way of thinking, this AdSense, should be the cornerstone of the micro-advertisers marketing plan.

Kirk Donovan

I am one who believes that one of the greatest dangers of advertising is not that of misleading people, but that of boring them to death!

--Leo Burnett

Kirk Donovan

Chapter Eleven
Get Your Head Out Of Your Ads

There's another important obstacle to advertising success. It creates waste in the millions of dollars. And it's produced some of the most offensive, ridiculous, unappealing ads in history. It is the <u>ego</u>.

One day, a radio sales rep told me an all-too-familiar story. On the previous day she met a potential client, a plastic surgeon, who had called her station inquiring about ad rates. He spent the first fifteen minutes of the conversation crying the blues over how much money he had wasted on advertising.

He bought expensive four color magazine ads and got absolutely no response. He tried newspaper advertising. He got some response, but not nearly enough to cover the cost. He spent money on cable television, to no avail.

"Please," he implored. "I'm at my wit's end. I can't afford to lose any more money!"

My sales rep, knowing that I could possibly help the frustrated physician, made a suggestion.

"Let me recommend someone who might be able to help guide you. An advertising consultant."

Instantly, he responded with a dogmatic air. "I don't need help. No one knows my business better than I do. I'm not going to pay someone to do something I can do myself for nothing."

What he was referring to was the fact that most media offer a 15% discount if the advertiser places the business through an advertising agency. They do that because there's less work for the media salesperson to do, since all the work is done by the agency. And the media wants more of the agency business. Most agencies handle more than just one account, so they develop "buying power."

Unfortunately, some media will use the 15% discount as a "hook" to close a potential client, even if they don't use an agency. This physician always did his own work and was always offered the discount. Why pay that money to someone else when he can pocket it?

He obviously needed to get new patients. <u>He</u> called the radio station to <u>begin</u> with. And he obviously didn't know what he was doing or he wouldn't have complained about all the money he wasted.

I Can Do It Myself!

What is it about people that makes them think they can be successful with advertising with absolutely <u>no</u> <u>knowledge</u> about advertising? No knowledge about the *language of advertising*. No knowledge about how to write copy that works. No knowledge of the methods and skills of media buying.

I know owners of very large businesses who spend thousands of dollars a month on expensive accountants. These highly trained, highly efficient CPAs know exactly what to do to keep their client's taxes at a minimum and his investments yielding the maximum.

That same business owner will spend thousands of dollars on corporate attorneys who are well educated and adept at protecting their client's legal interests.

Then, these astute business owners will spend $50,000 **a month** on advertising. They will have their office assistants call the television stations to place the television buy! And this uneducated assistant will meet with newspaper and radio salespeople to negotiate rates. She may be a terrific person, but does she know the language of advertising?

Then, the business owner will write a script and use his dull, plain voice to record the ad. Does <u>he</u> know that *language of advertising?*

In the case of the stumped surgeon, the one who "thought he could"…he no longer advertises. He tried radio for one month and said it didn't work!

When I heard this story, it prompted me to include a section in my lectures called *"Get Your Head Out of Your Ads*!"

One of the major reasons why 85% of all advertising is ineffective, or not as effective as it could be, is that a great many people who are doing it really <u>shouldn't</u> be doing it!

I had a media buyer tell me one day that she always recommended to her clients to do radio advertising in the Spring. She took me outside and said "See, look how beautiful it is out here! Everyone is listening to radio, not watching television."

I suggested that she look at the television research. If people aren't watching television in the Spring, why do all the networks use the Spring as one of their biggest ratings periods? The numbers may drop off in the summer months, with all the re-runs, but even then the average loss of audience is only about 10%. But the cost of advertising in the summer is less, compensating for the difference.

A major obstacle to success in just about *anything* in life is the ego. Relationships fail because people are too stubborn to communicate. Who likes to say they are wrong? Egos have caused more than one ugly war. And egos waste millions of dollars <u>each</u> <u>day</u> in this country on advertising.

How many ads have you seen or heard that featured the owner or manager of the business <u>in</u> the ad? Of course, you hear it all the time. You see a guy on television who is stiff, inarticulate and almost frightened. You hear a guy on radio who sounds like he's reading to you.

I tried to consult with an attorney who had been doing personal injury television ads for many years. He told me he didn't need me to negotiate his media because he had a secretary who could do it just as well.

I asked this secretary if she knew the Atlanta daytime cost-per-point. She had no clue what a cost-per-point was. I asked if she knew how to read a Bar Report.

The Bar Report is a service of The Arbitron Ratings Company. It is a monthly tabulation of television advertising in most major markets. It shows every business that ran television advertising during a specific period. It shows how many commercials they ran, the times the spots ran, and even the programs they ran in. It even shows the approximate amount of money they spent on the campaign. Pretty useful information for positioning yourself among the competition!

She had no idea what a Bar Report was. She had no concept of positioning. Yet, she knew as well as an "expert" how to negotiate media for her boss!

The fact is that he just didn't want to pay the media commission. But he didn't realize that if negotiated properly, the 15% commission fee could have been neutralized by getting 15% <u>more</u> commercials on the air. <u>If</u> it is done by someone who understands how to buy media.

Why is this so? Because most media rates are negotiable and knowledge is power. The more knowledge you have of the rates at any given time, the more negotiating power you have. The more knowledge you have of what your competition is doing, the more power you'll have in determining how to get your share of the business.

Don't let your wife, your sales manager, your golfing buddies or anyone else tell you how you should do your advertising. Get involved yourself. You and your agency should have total creative control in developing consistent and cohesive messages and buys.

What happened to the attorney who *thought he could*? He no longer runs television ads. He's even been sued by several television stations to recover their money! He should have kept his head out of his ads and turned it over to someone who knew what they were doing. He had to learn the hard way!

Ads are the cave art of the 20th Century.

--Marshall McLuhan

Kirk Donovan

Chapter Twelve
The 15% Myth

Negotiable media is a term referring to any media that has parameters in their pricing structure. For instance, a television station may show a price on their rate card of $1000 for a 30-second ad. If I offer $800 for that ad, and there is an availability, or *avail*, the station <u>may</u> sell it to me.

The only problem is that if another business comes along between the time I bought the ad and when it actually runs, and offers $900 for that same ad space, chances are that my spot will be "bumped" for the higher offer.

Herein lays the negotiability of advertising. The skill for the media buyer is in knowing, at any given time, where those parameters fall. It's a blend of being able to get a lower rate (but not to the point of losing the avail) and not prostituting the integrity of the station's rates.

Naturally, the advertising salesperson's job is to get the highest rate possible to look good for management, but still keep it as low as possible for the potential client to make the purchase. Their job is to "fill holes."

A good media salesperson learns exactly how much his potential client knows about media buying. The less the buyer knows the higher the rate will be. The buyer who understands the parameters negotiates more effectively.

These parameters change constantly. During the second and fourth quarters of the year, more advertisers want to be on the air.

These, of course, are the Spring and Christmas buying seasons when national advertising increases <u>and</u> local advertisers spend most of their ad dollars. More demand means less supply and less negotiability.

Political seasons are tough for media buyers because Federal law dictates that the political advertisers get the lowest rate the station has offered for any day-part during the previous three months. More demand, less supply, less negotiability.

During the first and third quarters, stations do everything they can to sell ads. More supply, less demand, more negotiability. And of course the lower the ratings of a station, the lower the demand. That means more negotiability.

Many years ago, long before I started selling radio advertising, negotiable media began offering a 15% commission to local advertisers as a "hook."

"Look," they would tell a potential client who is on the verge of buying. "If you sign the contract now, I'll give you the 15% discount. We'll call it *an in-house agency discount.*

The discount, called an *agency discount*, is for advertising agencies or media buyers who do the work. Those agencies put together the ad schedules, create the commercials, and give it to the stations "ready to run." That means less work for the station's salesperson. More time to be on the street selling! It was worth the 15% discount for the media.

But once it became a "hook," it became the fatal blow to a lot of micro-advertisers. Why pay an expert to do the placement when I can save the 15%?

As time went on, more and more advertisers found out about the discount and began demanding it. "If the guy next door gets it, so should I!"

Now, I would say that over 50% of all local advertising nationwide is created by the business themselves, rather than utilizing the services of a legitimate agency or consultant.

I can't count the number of times I lost a potential client because a radio or television station offered them a discount. And a huge percentage of those ran for just a few months, and then stopped. The station got their money, the client got his discount, but the advertising didn't work because the person doing the ads really didn't understand what they were doing.

Instead of paying a company which could probably do better creative and get better rates because of the combined buying power of *all* their clients, otherwise astute business owners will "do it themselves" to save the 15%.

For example, if you spend $10,000, you have the buying power of $10,000. But the agency might have a combined buying power of $100,000. Guess who has more negotiability?

Businesses that try to save the 15% don't have their head in their wallets. They have their head in their ads!

When I taught classes at Florida State University, I used to tell my graduating students what I considered to be one of the most important things they could hear at this stage of their lives. I told them that four years of college didn't mean that they were educated. It only means that they are <u>*educable*</u>.

College won't make you successful in any business. Law school doesn't teach you how to be a lawyer. It just teaches you the *language of law*. You have to take that knowledge and become a lawyer, using your own talents.

Medical school doesn't teach you how to be a doctor, it teaches you the *language of medicine*.

Understanding the language of advertising is an important first step in using AdSense.

Unfortunately, there are no requirements for being an advertising consultant. And because there are no enforceable codes governing ad agencies or consultants, there are a lot of people out there representing themselves as "experts." They are really <u>not</u> experts.

In every community there are huge numbers of people who get out of college, work a year or two selling for a local radio station or newspaper, and then open their doors as a "consultant."

I know a gentleman in Atlanta who worked for several years at a small newspaper, selling advertising. After about four years, he went to work for a small radio station selling ads. He did that for two years.

Then he came to me and asked my advice about him opening his own agency. He was very good at selling ads, but had very little experience writing ads. He knew nothing about television. He was a good talker, and a very nice guy. But what right did he have to take $10,000 or more <u>a month</u> from some small businessman and in good conscience tell him how to spend it? He's taking a real gamble with a lot of money…money that isn't his! The loss does not sting the consultant, only the client.

It's like going to Las Vegas and gambling with a lot of money, losing every dime, and going home happy. Only it's worse. The poor guy whose money was just thrown away <u>paid</u> the gambler to lose it!

How To Find the Right Help

If you're going to spend money on advertising, either learn how to do it or hire someone who knows how to do it. Don't just *think* you know what you're doing. Look beyond your ego and make decisions based on skill and knowledge...even if the 15% commission is causing you to do it yourself. It's an illusion if you end up losing much more than the 15% offered.

And if you're hiring someone to help you with your advertising, do a little research. Don't make your decision to hire someone based on how well you like them. That sounds ludicrous, but believe me, that's exactly why most consultants or agencies are hired.

If you hire an agency, let them offer their advice and suggestions. Don't just hire them to facilitate the ideas <u>you</u> have. They might have better ideas, or could possibly embellish your ideas.

I'm reminded of the story of a business owner who calls three advertising agencies to solicit their help. He asks all three agencies the same opening question.

"What time is it?"

The first guy said, "It's 2:30."

"I'll get back to you," the inquiring business owner said.

The second guy said, "I'll have to do some research and call you back."

The third guy said, "What time would you like it to be?" He was hired on the spot.

Find out how much experience they have in buying <u>all</u> media? How much is their buying power worth? How long have they had their current clients? What is their reputation with the media? What is their education level? What do they know about behavioral science? A knowledgeable buyer can save you much more than the 15% if they know what they are doing.

If you want to have a chance of falling into the 15% of advertising that is successful, you must first get your head out of your ads. That is until, of course, your head is filled with the knowledge, skill and experience necessary to make prudent decisions.

Kirk Donovan

There is an old saying that there are three kinds of lies in advertising…....big lies, white lies and statistics.

--Unknown author

Chapter Thirteen
Statistical Science of Advertising

The statistical science of advertising is the essence of the media business. It is the tool by which all media establish prices to charge for their services.

The size of a radio station's audience, for instance, is measured statistically by a *ratings company*. If a station gets high ratings, it has a large share of the radio audience. If it has low ratings, it doesn't have a big audience. More about radio later.

When I sold radio advertising early in my career, in a small Florida market, the ratings at my station fluctuated from good to mediocre. When the ratings were good, we were able to charge higher rates. But when ratings were lower, we would do everything we could to avoid mentioning ratings. "You live by the ratings, you die by the ratings!" was the edict.

I will give you a frame of reference by which rate decisions are based in most markets. Again, I'll use a radio station example. But first, let me explain that no micro-advertiser has enough money to reach everyone in their market every month. The best thing they can do is reach as many as they can efficiently. Unless you have enough money, you will always miss potential customers.

Let's assume there are ten radio stations in our sample market.

National advertisers that want to *penetrate* our market will go to the top 2 or 3 stations to place their client's money. The decision to make these buys is usually done far away by people who never even listened to radio in that market. The ad agencies or media placement services decide where to place their ads by looking at the ratings.

So how does the station establish the rates they charge for commercials? First the station decides how many commercials it wants to sell each hour. These are called *avails,* short for availabilities. Some stations call them *units.* Now, an hour is an hour, whether you're in New York City or Tallahassee, Florida. The average number of *avails* sold each hour is about 12 to 15 units, either 30 or 60 seconds. That means a minute in New York should cost a lot more than a minute in Tallahassee, simply because the audience is so much bigger.

The most simplified way of determining rate is by using a cost-per-thousand basis. In New York City, if your audience size at 10 o'clock in the morning is 1,500,000 people, and you want a $10 CPM, or cost-per-thousand, that commercial would cost $15,000.

$$\$15,000 \div 1,500,000 = .01$$
$$.01 \times 1000 \text{ (CPM)} = \$10 \text{ CPM}$$

If a station in Tallahassee, Florida reaches an average of 8,000 people and you want a CPM of $10, the rate would be $80 for the commercial.

$$\$80 \div 8,000 = .01$$
$$.01 \times 1000 \text{ (CPM)} = \$10 \text{ CPM}$$

Therefore, you can achieve the same cost-per-thousand in Tallahassee as you can in New York City, although you reach a lot more people in New York City. It can be just as cost effective.

Because there are a fixed number of messages sold each hour, radio and television rates are on a constant up-and-down fluctuation, based on *supply and demand.* The number of local avails is greater for the number six rated station than for the number one rated radio station, because national advertisers buy a bigger chunk of the total avails on the number one station. Therefore, the number six station has a greater supply of avails. Local rates should be lower.

More businesses want to buy the number one station because of its greater audience size. More demand means higher rates, once the avails begin to diminish. These factors are important when analyzing statistically the efficiency of most media buys.

Some businesses buy advertising on the lowest rated stations because the prices are so much lower. On the top rated station, you may get 5 spots for the budget you have to spend. But on the lowest rated station, you may get 50 spots for the same price. That's 50 lines in the water! But remember, you have to be where the fish are!

There's another way to say this. If an ad falls in the forest and there is no one around to hear it, does it make a noise?!

The statistical science of advertising is essential in determining whether or not you are being cost effective in your media placement. By determining audience sizes, and by learning the cost-per-thousand of other competing media, media can assign and justify rates.

Again, the higher the ratings or the more people the media reaches, the higher the rates will be. It is that station's reward for doing so well. And in most cases, *these* stations can establish the cost-per-thousand for their market.

Now, let's look at each of the major media. We will explore their strengths and weaknesses, and how each is *statistically* priced. You'll see how decisions are made in determining where billions of dollars are spent annually.

And you'll see that AdSense also plays an important role in the statistical science of advertising.

You can say the right thing about a product and nobody will listen. You've got to say it in a way that people will feel it in their gut. Because if they don't feel it, nothing will happen.

--William Bernbach

Chapter Fourteen
Radio Media

Late on the night on April 14, 1912, a young telegrapher sat high atop Wannemaker's Department Store in New York City. He was manning his post at the Marconi wireless station. He picked up an incredible message. "S.S. Titanic ran into iceberg…sinking fast."

Reporters, relatives and the curious descended on the store to receive reports from the young man with the "wireless fist." For three days and nights, the young man stuck to his post. President Taft ordered all the other wireless on the East Coast off the air, so that this channel would be free of interference.

The wireless operator was a young Russian emigrant of considerable talent, genius and foresight. His name was David Sarnoff. The disaster established the reliability and importance of wireless. But much more happened as a result of that somber night.

Sarnoff spent countless hours thinking about the significance of that fateful event. If simple dot-dash signals could be transmitted over thousands of miles, why can't more complex signals be transmitted as well?

The vibrations of music were just such signals. Sarnoff proposed a "radio music box" and outlined a plan of development which he believed would make it a "household utility." On that momentous night of April 14, 1912, radio was born.

The future "General" David Sarnoff made broadcast history as a pioneer, and later, as founder of the RCA Corporation and founder and Chairman of NBC, the National Broadcasting Company.

The first twelve years of my career were spent in radio. And prior to that, my parents were radio veterans from the "Golden Days of Radio." For much of my early career, radio advertising baffled me. For some businesses, it was a costly mistake. For some, the return was much greater than the investment. I was perplexed. What was the secret of making radio effective?

It's obvious the audience is there. Almost 99% of U.S. households have at least one radio, and the average American household has 5.9 sets. Within one week's time, radio reaches 95.8% of all people age 12 and over.

Radio is a selective medium. That means there are many different types of music or talk formats, differentiated program formats appealing to various consumer segments. The firm that measures these many radio audiences is called Arbitron Research Company.

By learning to read an Arbitron Research Report on your market, you can determine a narrow age group, male or female dominated audiences, and even lifestyles of audiences.

Another research report, Scarborough, measures everything from what kinds of cars an audience prefers, to when their next refrigerator might be purchased.

So, research tells us audience sizes. Now, how does a station determine rates? First, they have to decide how much inventory they have to sell.

Radio ads are sold as "units," primarily 30 or 60 seconds in length. These units are sold in "day-parts." Any spots falling between 5:30 am and 10 am are in the *morning drive* day-part.

Midday falls between 10 a.m. and 3 p.m., and the 3 p.m. to 7 p.m. day-part is called *afternoon drive*.

These terms came about in the 1960s when most people had only AM radios, and AM stations were "king." With the advent, and eventual dominance, of FM signals, more radios went into the workplace.

These stronger signals went through concrete and weren't affected by fluorescent lights...the doom of AM radio. The once significant gap in audience size from morning to midday to afternoons narrowed considerably. In some cases, midday even gets <u>higher</u> ratings.

The other day-parts are nighttime, overnights and weekends.

At most stations, they all experience sharp drops in audience size during these times.

Even though the gap has narrowed, advertisers still desire morning and afternoon drive times the most. But how many minutes are there to sell during these coveted times?

If a radio station averages 12 minutes of advertising per hour, that means they have 96 minutes of "prime" advertising time over a period of eight hours. That leaves 192 additional minutes available to sell to advertisers for the remaining 16 hours of the day.

The job of a radio station sales manager is to sell as many total units as possible. *Packages* are suggested, usually consisting of spots in every day-part.

During my radio advertising sales days, we were trained to say, "People who work during the night spend money too!" A sales manager has to creatively convince advertisers to spread their money around. That fills the holes.

Sometimes they'll include "value-added" items to their packages. *Remotes* are live broadcasts from an advertiser's location. A popular disc jockey will show up, armed with free hats, T-shirts, food and refreshments. They will urge people to get in their cars and come down to meet them.

So a station may offer a package which includes five morning drive spots, five midday spots, five afternoon drive spots, five nighttime spots and a remote broadcast . . . all for a specified amount of money.

Or the station may offer you the sponsorship of a morning traffic report. The price may be higher than normal morning drive rates, but it's justified since you get an additional "billboard."

For example... *this message is brought to you by Bob's Downtown Clothiers.*

The question you must ask is "how much impact can value-added have?" If the purpose of advertising is to simply create an image by "keeping your name out there," then these short mentions are justified.

But if each message has to be used to entice a response, it can't be easily done in the five to ten seconds that *billboards* are usually comprised of.

There are really only two ways to use radio advertising successfully. The first is a strategic campaign. In this method, you should run a lot of commercials over a short period of time. A good strategic campaign would utilize about 25 to 30 commercials over a period of one or two weeks.

The second way to do radio advertising is to run fewer spots, between five and ten per week, over a long period of time. This is called a maintenance schedule. In this campaign, the purpose is to just "keep your name out there." This is where realistic expectations come into play.

If you're having a sale to get rid of a large inventory that needs to me moved, you'd probably discount the price and put a limit on the time in which the public can get the savings. This is creating an "urgency."

For instance, a furniture store may have twenty new rocking chairs at a savings of 20%. "But hurry…these rockers won't last long at this price, and this sale ends Saturday."

If this is your "hook," but you run just 5 commercials in one week to announce it, you probably won't get the kind of results you expect. A lot of businesses will do this, sell only a few rockers, and think that radio advertising doesn't work.

Using the same furniture store, if you run a maintenance, or institutional, message, without a hook, and run 25 spots in a week, you probably won't get good results either. The message should have a "call to action" if you expect an immediate response. Everyone is not shopping for furniture every day.

An institutional message has a goal of letting prospective

furniture buyers know that when the time comes for them to look for furniture, they should remember your name. A strategic message says "even if you don't need furniture right now, <u>this</u> rocking chair at <u>this</u> price is hard to pass up."

Advertising can satisfy the need of a consumer in short order, if you offer the product they need, when they need it, at a competitive price. But advertising can also <u>create</u> a need. It can make a person who never knew they needed a "widget" think they need that widget. Spontaneity produces a <u>lot</u> of revenue in this country, usually with lower priced objects.

Advertising campaigns have to rely on frequency, or the number of times a person hears your message. A person needs to hear your message up to ten times before they will retain the information.

It is important to note that there is a big difference between *listening* and *hearing*. You usually have the radio on in your car. Your mind is on traffic, or what you have to do at work, or your date last night. The radio is loud, and you *hear* the commercials, but you aren't actively *listening* to the content of the message. But if you hear the same message several times, and something about the ad catches your interest, you may eventually listen to it.

Radio sales reps tell me all the time, based on the research, how many "listeners" they have in morning drive. I tell them that they don't have that many "listeners." They have that many "hearers."

Listening requires conscious involvement. It is up to the creativity of the message to get them to listen.

But even if you <u>are</u> listening to a message, but you aren't in the market for what the message offers, you still *note* the name of the company. If the time ever comes that you are in need of the product the company offers, hopefully you'll remember that company's name…but only if you have enough *notations* in your memory from their commercials. The chance of that happening depends on the consistency of the ad campaign over a long period of time without becoming rhetorical or resilient.

Advertising also has to rely on reach, which equals how many different people hear your message each time your spot runs. A successful campaign uses a combination of reach and frequency. Unfortunately, it takes a great amount of money to get an appreciable return, but if the audience is chosen properly, and the message does what it is supposed to do, the payoff could be profitable. The question becomes "do you have enough money and time to wait for that payoff?"

What if you have a business on the north side of town and decide to run a radio schedule which reaches the entire town and beyond? Is it worth spending money on the entire marketplace, knowing that the only people who would potentially respond are in your area? It depends.

First, are you the only business in town that offers what you do? If so, people <u>will</u> drive across town to find you. But there are few businesses that hold exclusive rights to a product line.

For example, a small to medium size market might have four or five Ford dealers, but only one BMW dealer. If you want a BMW, you will drive as far as you have to. You'll only pass the other four Ford dealers if you think the one farthest from you has more inventory or lower prices.

Otherwise, you have to determine if there are enough people in your area who can respond to your message to make it profitable. Or, and this sounds pretentious, put another location on the other side of town and share the ad costs. One of the reasons so many companies have multiple locations in major cities is to diffuse the advertising costs in a competitive marketplace. This synergistic concept paved the way for "chain stores."

The only problem is you might not have enough money to open another location. There have been many well run businesses with excellent products or services that go bankrupt, losing to well financed companies with inferior products or services. This is the nature of the *business survival of the fittest.*

The advantages of radio are numerous. A radio station usually reaches a large number of people. And among all major media, radio is the best at targeting particular audiences. If you're appealing to people over 50, there are usually only one or two stations that program to that demographic. You can target your message specifically to that group.

Another advantage to using radio is that just about everyone listens to it sometime during the day.

And radio is probably the easiest media to use. Newspaper and television ads are expensive to produce, and time consuming. It doesn't take that much time or money to produce a radio ad.

What are radio's disadvantages? Well, it's the only major media that people utilize while doing something else. When you're watching television, you're focused on the television. When you're reading a newspaper, you're <u>reading</u> the newspaper. But when you're listening to the radio, you're usually driving or working. It does not hold your attention like the other media do. It doesn't have the selective visual impact of television or print.

Another disadvantage is that if you have a broad customer base, you'll need to buy more than one station. That can get expensive.

Most people listen to more than one station. *Button pushers* pass up the advertising and go to another "favorite" station to find music. Your potential audience decreases when the music goes off and your message comes on.

So if you have a large enough budget, radio is best used in conjunction with other media. This is called a *media mix*.

Redundancy is a blend of more than one sense. If you see something visually, then hear it, chances are greater that you'll remember the message.

Whereas the future of print advertising and television advertising is nebulous in the fast-changing environment of entertainment choices, radio isn't going anywhere. As the internet grows, our television habits and sources for news and information are being redirected. But most people will still use the radio alarm to wake up, listen to the traffic and weather reports, and listen while driving their cars.

Even with the advent of music for car tape players and C.D. players, an industry which generates billions of dollars a year, the effect on radio listenership is minimal.

How you utilize radio in your advertising plan will determine the potential for success or the heartache of failure.

Advertising is salesmanship in print. Its principles are the principles of salesmanship. The only purpose of advertising is to make sales.

--Claude Hopkins

Chapter Fifteen
Newspaper Advertising

I had always heard that Benjamin Franklin was the first person to introduce advertising to the Americas. Actually, the concept of advertising had already been thriving in England since the 1600s.

The very first advertisement in English was written by a gentleman named William Claxton in 1477. He was trying to sell a new book of prayer that he had published in Westminster Abbey.

The earliest ads were posters and broadsides nailed to post offices and courthouses. But by the end of the American Revolution, advertising was here and already established. Even Paul Revere demonstrated skills of copy writing in 1768 in an ad selling his own brand of false teeth;

"Whereas many Persons are so unfortunate as to lose their fore-teeth by Accident, and otherways, to their great detriment not only in looks, but speaking both in Public and Private. This is to Inform all such, that they may have them replaced with artificial Ones that look as well as the Natural, and answers the End of Speaking to all Intents, by Paul Revere, Goldsmith, near the Head of Dr. Clarke's Wharf, Boston."

The first daily newspaper was published in Philadelphia, courtesy of a part-time printer named Benjamin Franklin. He was the first creative publisher to use pictures to break up blocks of copy. He was also the first to use a lot of white space around centered headlines. The first New York daily newspaper was begun in 1785.

During the first half of the Republic, there was really no need to advertise. Most of the country lived on farms, where just about everything a family needed was produced. Householders sold what small surplus there was after the family met its needs. This surplus was the small amount of money the ads were appealing to. Most of it went for coffee, salt, hardware, clothes and tools. (Advertising in America, The First 200 Years, Harry N. Abrams, Inc., New York, 1990)

When economic conditions began to change, advertising as we know it began in earnest. Newspapers began to grow as we moved Westward in an effort to keep the new pioneers informed about what was going on back east. The age of Mass Communication began slowly and deliberately.

The use of newspapers for advertising goes back generations, and has become ingrained in the American psyche. As the economy grew, department stores, carrying everything a homeowner could wish for, began to sprout up. The only way these stores had to announce their wares was through newspaper advertising.

Today, nearly 25% of all advertising expenditures are still spent in newspaper.

So what about your business? When you're spending your money to try to move an audience to action, one of the first things you should look at is the credibility of the medium. Newspapers, being centuries old, have a proven reputation for credibility.

As the Communication Age progressed, people's hunger for information increased. Rather than wait weeks or months to receive information, our information now comes through the newspaper in detail the next day, or in some cases, the day the event occurs.

So, what are the advantages of this storied medium to the advertiser? Should you consider it in your advertising mix? Is it as cost effective as it used to be? How big a gamble is it? And does it work better for some types of business than others?

The first thing that newspaper advertising offers is the mass audience, and the variety of consumers it reaches. Among its loyal readers, it enjoys a high degree of familiarity, acceptance and respect.

Another thing that makes newspaper advertising a strong choice is that you can carry a picture of your product or service being offered. It is a tangible medium. Ads and coupons can be cut out and brought to the advertisers so they can actually see the result of the expenditure.

And the audience who reads the newspaper is as varied as our lifestyles. The average entrepreneur will try to check the business page on a regular basis to see what his competitors are doing, to watch for trends in the ever-changing economy and to check investments.

The average American tries to keep up on sensational world events and local events. Whereas radio and television give the audience a capsule of events, the newspaper can describe the event in more detail.

The global community and mass communication created in our society a desire to be the best, the fastest, the strongest, the most agile. And if we can't achieve these things individually, we idolize the people who can. This hunger for success manifested itself into a huge industry…the sports business.

The Sports Page attracts people who can't watch each game or attend each event they desire, but have a passion to find out if their favorite team won. And they want to discern every statistic imaginable on their favorite team.

The accessibility of television and movies in the Mass Communication Age created another section in the newspaper…the Entertainment Page. Without it we wouldn't know what time the movie starts, what time our favorite television show airs or what concerts and plays are in town.

Automobile, real estate, job employment and classified ads have special sections in most newspapers. And the need for knowing what is happening with our neighbors and friends created the Social Pages. And of course, our opinions are shaped by essays on the Editorial Pages.

By attracting such a diverse audience, newspaper advertising could target its salient audiences more effectively. But could the advancement of mass communication contribute to the possible demise of the vehicle that began it all?

Newspaper circulation is definitely decreasing in our society. Today's modern family, with two providers, has very little time to read the newspaper like our ancestors did. Since the 1980s, American newspapers began going out of business as fast as Mom & Pop restaurants. Most large American cities had a morning and afternoon edition.

Today, the afternoon editions are rare. According to the Radio Advertising Bureau, a typical reader spends less than 40 minutes with the newspaper. That will give you barely enough time to read the sections you want, much less spend time looking at the ads.

Along with decreasing circulation, newspaper rates have continued to increase, due to the increasing costs of paper, production and delivery. But it still commands a great share of the total advertising expenditures. The popularity of this medium has created a great clutter of ads. The average advertising content today is 62% for a daily newspaper and 68% on Sunday.

So the enterprising newspaper sales representative will try to sell you a larger ad in order to "stand out." The problem is that larger ads don't always deliver enough of an increase in reach to justify the increase in cost.

Another disadvantage of newspaper advertising is that most newspapers offer little in the way of competitive separation, giving a distinct sales advantage to the advertiser who can offer the better price.

In addition, one of the primary targets for most advertisers, the 18-34 consumers, seldom sees the daily newspaper. Studies show that they are much more prone to get their information from electronic media.

A great disadvantage to the advertiser is something the newspapers sell as an advantage. If you're trying to advertise just one time, the rate you are charged is called an "open rate." It's the most expensive rate in the newspaper. In order to get a better rate; you have to agree to a long-term contract, or a commitment to a large number of inches over a period of time, usually a year.

But what if the ad doesn't work? What if the expense of running the ad isn't covered by the results you get from the ad? You're stuck with a long-term contract. And if you don't live up to your original commitment, you are "short rated." The newspaper will go back to the original rate you would have been charged had you run a shorter commitment, and you will owe them the difference. Bad enough it didn't work, now you have to shell out <u>more</u> money!

I've seen many businesses suffer over the years because their newspaper advertising didn't work, and they were obligated for more money.

Automobile advertising makes up for a great amount of newspaper revenue. Our society has been trained over the years to go to the classified section of our newspaper to compare prices and see what local dealers have to offer.

A full-page color ad in the local newspaper of a major city, without a contract commitment, would cost about $20,000 or more. If a dealer signs a contract that he will run that ad once or twice a week for a year, the cost of the same ad could get as low as $9000. Quite a difference!

But, even with a low contract rate, the ad that costs $9000 would have to result in selling nearly 50 cars to make it a worthwhile investment. The ad comes out one day, and the dealer must sell 50 cars in that day to be profitable. Imagine how many cars the dealer would have to sell with a $20,000 ad. It would be almost impossible to be successful.

Newspaper advertising costs more to reach each person than television or radio.

And why is it that 20% of the people in the market for a car today go to the automobile classified section of the newspaper, but car dealers spend about 80% of their overall budgets on the medium? Is it because every other dealer is in there? Do we buy the classifieds out of fear?

Another thing to take into consideration is that market conditions change constantly, weather factors can create a successful or unsuccessful sales day, or that a competing dealer might have an ad right next to yours one day with lower prices on every car. That day would probably be considered a loss.

So, what type of advertisers should be in the newspaper? How do you increase your chances for success? There are categories of business that have traditionally advertised in the newspaper, such as the aforementioned automobile advertiser.

One of the first categories was department stores. John Wannemaker's Department Store in New York City built its success with newspaper ads. Even back then, in the early 1900s, he stated that half of his advertising worked and half didn't!

And to follow the tradition, department stores of today have dominated newspaper advertising. Just look at the full page ads announcing a "White Sale" at your local department store. Most newspapers are full of them at least one day a week, if not more.

Tires and auto parts have probably always been advertised in the Sports Page of your local newspaper on Saturday, because men buy tires and auto parts, and men will spend more time on the Sports Page.

Furniture stores have found newspaper pages to be very effective to announce their wares, especially since they can show pictures. And of course, grocery stores have a long tradition of newspaper advertising.

Newspaper advertising is still a solid choice for advertising, and it will be for a long time. But as electronic communication and technology continues to advance, and as our society continues to offer other choices to get our information in a time-limited environment, the newspaper industry must find other ways to make their advertising costs more effective.

Newspapers will always be around, but the success of the industry in dominating advertising expenditures may suffer.

Kirk Donovan

Many a small thing has been made large by the right kind of advertising.

---Mark Twain

Kirk Donovan

Chapter Sixteen
Television Advertising

"Television will enormously enlarge the eye's range, and, like radio, will advertise to the Elsewhere."   *E.B. White—1938 lecture*

There is much debate over who invented television. The beginning of the 20th century was a time when the brilliant minds of scientific discovery prospered. Alexander Graham Bell had recently invented the telephone. Gugliamo Marconi astonished the skeptics in 1899 by receiving the first radio signal –the letter "S" – in Newfoundland. The signal was sent from the other side of the Atlantic.

Thomas Edison continued to amaze the world with his inventions—the electric light bulb, the phonograph, the box camera and pictures with motion.

An article in the New York Daily News in early 1904 reported that a German scientist, Professor Arthur Korn, talked "very modestly of 'televista,'" the name he had given his 'seeing by wire' invention. The word television comes from the ancient Greek and Latin roots for "far off" and "see."

The article read, "Now that the photo-telegraph is on the eve of being introduced into general practice, we are informed of some similar inventions in the same field, all of which tend to achieve some step toward the solution of the problem of television."

Dr. Korn had transmitted a photograph by way of a telegraphic circuit.

In 1884, a 24 year-old German inventor, Paul Nipkow, had shown that television was feasible. He devised a perforated disc through which images could be scanned by mechanical means; a rotating wheel that first broke down and then reconstructed the image.

In the early 1920s, while radio began to flourish, experiments continued in the effort of marrying sound and vision.

John Logie Baird, a Scottish tinkerer in the field of electronics, transmitted the first moving image…shades of light and shade barely recognizable as a face. His apparatus was adopted by the Germans and the young British Broadcasting Company, or the BBC. Many believe that his early work qualifies him for the title of the "inventor" of television.

Meanwhile, in the United States, Charles Francis Jenkins was doing similar work. As early as 1923, he transmitted a picture of President Warren G. Harding by wireless from Washington D.C. to Philadelphia, Pennsylvania.

In 1924, at a farm in Idaho, a young man named Philo Taylor Farnsworth had worked out the concepts of a television system. His first application for a patent for his "cathode ray tube" was made on

January 7, 1927.

These were the pioneers of television. The first commercial television station, WNBT in New York, began broadcasts to about 4700 TV set owners in 1941. Less than 50 years later, there were over 1250 television stations and 830 cable systems in the United States. Today, those numbers shrink in comparison.

Today, television has overtaken all other forms of media in its power and impact. In the 1940s, families would sit down with their favorite beverage and stare at their radio with undivided attention. Do they do that today?

Television, with its sight and sound and motion, is the most intrusive form of media today. Every radio station has its own distinct audience demographics, but a television station reaches every conceivable demographic during the course of a day.

The sources for the micro-advertiser's advertising expenditures on television can be broken down into two categories. The first is the local over-the-air network affiliates and independent commercial channels. The second method is to use local cable channels.

Network affiliates usually have the largest audiences. These stations carry network programming during the most viewed day-parts, usually comprising of early morning new programs, dinnertime news hours and the "prime time" period of 8 p.m. until 11 p.m.

During these high profile times, the station receives and transmits signals originating from network headquarters. Each program has a certain number of local availabilities called "local breaks." These are obviously the most expensive spots available on the station because there are so few of them and they reach the largest number of people.

The cost of a spot in these areas can reach into thousands of dollars, which makes it unaffordable to many micro-advertisers. These spots are usually purchased by the businesses that group together their ad budgets. For instance, a local Dodge dealer can't afford a prime time spot, but the Dodge dealer group <u>can</u> afford it.

A single restaurant may not be able to afford these time slots, but a franchise group of dozens of restaurants <u>can</u> afford it.

The micro-advertiser basically "fills in the holes." These time slots don't reach nearly as many people as prime time, but even smaller television audiences can have a lot of impact. These advertisers can't afford a spot in the National news, but may be able to afford a spot in the 6 p.m. and 11 p.m. local newscasts.

There are plenty of availabilities during daytime, late night and weekend programming. These are the areas where television stations realize huge profits.

Independent stations have a great deal more time to sell than local network stations. These stations carry very little, if any, national programming. They show an abundance of sitcom reruns, specials and movies.

Whereas a network station might offer seven or eight local avails during the 9 p.m. till 10 p.m. time period, an independent station with no national time slots could sell up to 20 commercials to local advertisers during the same period. With a larger supply of avails on an independent station, the rates can be more affordable to the small advertiser.

The other source of advertising in high profile areas comes from local cable providers. The stations offered are the CNNs and other news channels, the A&E's, the Discovery Channels, the History Channels, the Lifetime Channels, the music channels like MTV and VH-1, the childrens channels like Nickelodeon and The Cartoon Network, the classic movie channels, the sports channels and many more.

These networks and their enormous amount of avails can target a narrow group of demographics and lifestyles. The only problem is the small number of viewers these networks attract at any given time.

Even in prime time, these networks attract only a small sliver of the available audience. So if a local Pontiac dealer runs a cable ad, there is something very important to consider. Remember, only 1% of the audience is in the market for a car on any given day. And Pontiac only attracts about 5% of the automobile industry. That means that only 5% of 1% of the viewing audience would potentially respond to your commercial. What kind of impact could you expect by reaching 5% of 1% of a small sliver of audience? Your chances are rather slim.

How are ad costs determined? For a thirty-second spot on television, there are several determinants. First is the size of the audience within your coverage area. Next is the audience size for a particular station, and for a particular show.

Another determinant is the number of ads you buy over a period of time. It just makes sense that a station will charge a higher price to a client that buys one spot, as opposed to a 200 or 300 spot buy. This is called "packaging." The advantage to the television station is to sell some of its ad slots in poor time periods. What it does for the advertiser is reduce the average cost per spot significantly.

Both the network stations and the cable stations define their basic service by geography. This coverage area is called the area of dominant influence, or ADI. Networks and most independent stations cover a larger area than most cable stations, but the advantage of cable is that it can target a more defined area.

One cable provider can break down their advertiser's coverage by community. Of course, the audience size diminishes greatly, but it is narrowed down to a specific geographical location. If you sell tires at a store that is located only on the north side of town, why would you want to reach people on the south side of town who have their own local tire stores?

How does a television station measure its audience size in order to determine rates? They do it by measuring terms like reach, frequency, rating and share. Here are some things you need to know when buying television advertising.

A station's rating or share is determined by independent survey firms. The best known of these firms is the Nielsen Research Company.

A rating is the audience size shown as a percentage of the total population. A rating point constitutes 1% of the households using television. The share of audience is usually expressed as a percentage of TVs that are tuned to a specific channel at a particular time out of all TVs in the coverage area. For instance, a share of 15 simply means that 15% of the televisions in the market area are watching a particular channel at a particular time.

Television audience potential is based on households using television, or HUT levels, and persons using television, or PUT levels.

Gross impressions are the total audience of average quarter hour persons available for the total number of commercials in any given schedule.

Gross rating points (GRPs) are the total of all rating points gained for a given schedule.

Finally, there is cost per rating point and cost per thousand. CPR is the cost of reaching 1% of the population in a given age group.

Cost per thousand is the price of delivering 1000 gross impressions.

There are two other things to learn if you are trying to buy an effective media schedule. Frequency is the average number of times a person has the opportunity to see your commercial.

Reach is the number of people who are expected to see an ad on a station in a given time period, such as a week or a month. It is the unduplicated number of homes who might see the ad at least once.

So if 500,000 households are exposed to a one week ad campaign, and there is a net reach of 70,000 unduplicated households, your frequency would be 7.1. That means the average TV viewer will see your commercial 7.1 times over the week.

These numbers can be confusing and overwhelming to the television advertiser, but they are the only determinants available to gauge the price effectiveness of an ad campaign.

You need to learn and understand these terms. Don't act like you know it. Ask your media representatives to teach you.

T.V. Advantages

So what are the major advantages to television advertising? First, television reaches large segments of your potential audience at the local level.

Television offers the lowest cost to reach each person, according to USA Today, a print medium!

Statistics show that adults have 29.4 hours of free time a week. We spend 2.8 hour on reading. That includes books, newspapers, magazines and all the other printed material we have to disseminate each week.

We spend 2.7 hours on our hobbies and only .4 hours listening to radio.

But with television, we spend an average of 15 hours a week! The average American male spends 3 hours 40 minutes a day with television, while the average American female spends 4 hours 30 minutes a day.

To further enhance the power of television as an advertising medium, listen to this statistic: The top 100 advertisers in the country spend 80% of their ad budgets on television.

As a comparison to radio, the top radio station in any market delivers less than 2% of the adults at any given time, while just one local newscast reaches from 17% to 40% of adults.

Television is also unbeatable at appealing to the emotions. Television spots can combine sight, action, color and sound to leave an impression with impact, something no other major media can boast.

There is also a certain aura of prestige that accompanies being seen on television, if the message is properly portrayed.

And television offers advertisers the opportunity to reach limited demographic groups, enabling them to target their message to their potential audience. For instance, stock brokerage firms would reach a salient audience on Fox News, CNBC or MSNBC.

The disadvantages? Well your chances for reaching a sizeable audience outside your market area are enormous because of television's reach.

If a micro advertiser can't afford to buy a lot of frequency, his message may get lost in the clutter of other ads. In many cases, TV advertising loses its impact if an advertiser cannot buy reach and frequency. You have to commit to a long term campaign to see appreciable results.

This is where realistic expectations come into play. If you can't afford frequency over a short period, you should expect to spend money over a long period to see the success of your expenditure. Unfortunately, not a lot of small businesses can afford to spend that much money without seeing immediate results.

The production of the ad itself can be cost prohibitive. Some spots may cost thousands of dollars to produce, <u>before</u> it even gets on the air!

And probably the most frustrating disadvantage was created by the invention of the remote control. All the ratings and shares of a particular program in a particular day-part means nothing if the audience switches to another station during your commercial.

The explosion of programming choices and channel availability will continue to fragment television audiences. Technology, and the advent of the home computer, will certainly change the landscape of television and will produce a lesser impact from your advertising dollars.

As the Father of Television News, Edward R. Murrow, said of television, "The instrument can teach, it can illuminate; yes it can even inspire. But it can do those things only to the extent that those humans are determined to use it to those ends. Otherwise, it is merely lights and wires in a box."

Will it increase your knowledge and understanding of the world around us? Or will it become the push-button opiate? As they say in television…tune in next week.

Promise, large promise, is the soul of an advertisement.

--Samuel Johnson, English author

Chapter Seventeen
Paralinguistics

I was listening to a radio ad for a car dealer recently and heard the announcer say "…and you keep rebate!"

And you keep rebate?! When you look at a newspaper ad, you'd probably see this expressed in a starburst with the words "You Keep Rebate!"

Some radio station announcer was given the assignment to write an ad for the car dealer. He was given a newspaper ad as a fact sheet. I know. I spent my early radio career doing just that.

When the announcer saw "You keep rebate," he wrote it into his script. But if you were speaking to someone, you would say "You keep _the_ rebates." This announcer isn't speaking to you. He's _reading_ to you.

It's difficult enough for your ad to stand out among the clutter of other canned ads, disc jockey's ramblings, and all the other noise on a radio or television station without hearing someone read to you.

Let me reiterate one important point. No one turns on the radio to listen to commercials. Aside from the Super Bowl telecasts, no one turns on a television to watch the ads. We don't like to be the recipients of advertising messages.

Advertisers spend good money for their ads to be heard or seen. Your ad has to cut through the clutter.

Remember, there's a very big difference between "hearing" and "listening." You "hear" auditory sounds. "Listening" requires your *attention* and possible *retention*.

If you hear an ad that sounds like someone is reading to you, what do you think are the chances for you to be drawn to attention? The odds are greatly diminished.

Why does the announcer in our example sound like he is reading to you? Because he <u>is</u> reading! A script is a series of words and thoughts that have been written down on a sheet of paper.

This is very important. We write like we read, and we read like we write, but we don't <u>speak</u> like we read or write.

"You keep rebate" was written down for someone to *read* it. But we wouldn't <u>say</u> it to someone that way.

So, if you speak words that have been written, you would sound like you were reading. It's only natural. But how do good announcers read scripts and make them sound like they're making the words up as they go? It's with the understanding of paralinguistics.

Paralinguistics is a form of nonverbal communication that has to do with the _way_ words and thoughts are spoken.

There's nothing more annoying than having an ad read "at" you. Take situations in which two people are talking to each other leading up to the "sell" of the product they are advertising.

"Honey," the man says. "I think we should get out of the house this weekend."

"O.K. Where do you want to go?"

"Well, I heard about a great new restaurant. It is called Angelo's. They have great food."

"Great food! That's what I'm in the mood for. What a great idea!"

Pretty lame. But you hear ads like this all the time. Would you speak to your spouse like that?

And if the script weren't bad enough, the people doing the script are <u>reading</u> to you. It is difficult enough for advertising to work without making spots sound so bad.

So how can paralinguistics help? We speak using a language different than our written vocabulary. Our spoken language is filled with slangs, dialects and nonfluencies.

A slang is a nonstandard vocabulary of a culture or subculture, consisting of figures of speech marked by spontaneity.

In the South we say "ya'll." Up North we say "you'se guys."

A dialect is a regional variety of a language distinguished by pronunciation, grammar or vocabulary.

A nonfluency is a nonverbal communication term referring to a stutter, a pause or a repetition of words. Nonfluencies are the *natural* methods by which we express our thoughts in words.

We use nonfluencies in our speech constantly.

For instance, a script could be written as follows:

"Weekends are for enjoyment. You work hard all week. Why not take the family out this weekend for boating, biking, fishing or picnicking at Lake Lanier Resort?"

That seems easy to read. It sounds like something you'd read in a brochure. Now, make it sound like you're making it up as you go, adding some nonfluencies.

"Ya know, weekends are for enjoyment."

"Ya know" is a nonfluency, something you added to personalize the statement…like "yeah" instead of "yes."

"Why not take the family out this weekend for boating… (pause)…biking…(pause)…fishing…(pause)…even picnicking… (pause)…at Lake Lanier Resort?"

In writing, and when we read, we're taught that a comma is a signal to pause. A period is a signal to stop. But when we speak, we can ignore these principles.

Read this out loud.

"Imagine seeing the world through the wide window of an Amtrak Train. Relax as you see tremendous mountains and gentle streams. Explore cities so big and beautiful, they take your breath away!"

Now, follow the way we would probably "say" these lines.

"Imagine…(pause)…seeing the world through the wide window…(pause)…of an Amtrak Train. Relax…(pause)…as you see tremendous mountains…(pause)…and gentle streams…(pause)…and explore cities and towns and sights so big and beautiful…(pause)… they…(pause)…take…(pause)…your…(pause)…<u>breath</u> away!"

There's a lot of pauses where we see no commas, and even a place where we continue when we've seen a period. It's O.K. It's paralinguistics!

I'll continue to use this Amtrak copy to help you through, but first let me describe some things you need to know about paralinguistics.

Paralinguistics requires good voice and diction.

A good voice is clear, resonant, and has adequate breath control. It has a clear, understandable rate of speech, and an appropriate pitch level.

Articulation means we are producing individual sounds clearly. Enunciation produces linked sounds clearly, as in words. Diction means we are producing both sounds and ideas clearly.

Paralinguistics is how we use things like articulation, pitch, loudness, rate and quality of voice and diction to communicate messages <u>beyond</u> words and sentences.

Vocal qualities have been proven to indicate our moods, our attitudes, our state of health, even our self-esteem.

It's said that lasting first impressions are formed within minutes of an encounter. When a listener can't see all the nonverbal characteristics that make up credibility, when the voice is the <u>only</u> qualifier of these first impressions, it is mandatory that the voice use proper paralinguistics to identify that credibility.

One of the important elements of good speech is pitch. Pitch has to do with changing voice levels as you speak. The pitch of your voice helps determine the meaning behind your words.

Take a word as simple as "yes." Let me ask you a question. Would you like to go?

Now, answer out loud saying the word "yes" as if you <u>really do</u> want to go.

Now say it as if you <u>will</u> go, but don't really care one way or another.

Now say it like you really don't want to go, but I have bullied you into it.

Hear the pitch changes?

Try this exercise now. Say the words "I didn't do that." Say it first like you would normally say it, sort of matter-of-fact in your delivery. "<u>I</u> didn't do <u>that</u>."

Now say it defensively, like I've accused you of it before. "I didn't <u>do</u> that!"

Now say it like you are angry for bringing it up again. "<u>I</u> <u>didn't</u> <u>do</u> <u>that</u>!"

In sex, look how the same words have different meanings depending on how these two words are delivered.

"Don't. Stop!"

Or, "Don't stop!"

An argumentative tone of voice is emphasized by using accentuated elements of pitch.

Loudness is another form of paralinguistics which can indicate mood or create tension. Loudness is the perception or the degree of force with which a sound is produced.

First, speak each of these sentences softly. Then, using the underlined words, increase loudness.

Don't do <u>that</u>.

Leave me <u>alone</u>.

<u>Give</u> it to me.

Get <u>out</u> of here.

I <u>love</u> you.

See how loudness can affect meaning, sincerity, sarcasm or

emphasis.

Nonfluencies are also used in the rate of speech. Rate is the number of words per minute one speaks.

Speech phrasing is forming a group of spoken words that constitute a meaningful unit and is surrounded by pauses. If someone speaks too fast, they lose credibility. The same holds true if someone is hesitant in their speech.

Syllabic stress is the emphasis on a given syllable.

Let's go back to our Amtrak script. When we write words like "big" and "beautiful" we know their impact in our minds. But when we read the words out loud, we just *say* the words.

As an instructor in paralinguistics for over 15 years at the Atlanta Broadcast Institute, I had hundreds of people with <u>good</u> voices read the Amtrak script. In almost all cases, they said the word "big" the same way they said the word "beautiful."

But there is a significant difference between the words.

Take the time to say these words like they are imagined. "Big" is

BIG!

You stretch the "i" and you say it with force.

The word beautiful is very different. You speak it softer and more deliberately.

"<u>Beau</u>-ti-ful." You stretch the letters "beau" and say it softly.

Write these words on a sheet of paper and ask someone to read them. I'll bet they will say each word using the same emphasis. That's because they are reading words that have been written down.

Now, get them to <u>express</u> the words. See the difference?

Now, say these words using extenuated rate of speech, proper pitch, and stressing the loudness or softness of the words. I'll write it down the way you would say it, rather than the way you would read it. Sometimes that helps when writing a script.

"Imagine…seeing the world through the <u>wide</u> (stress the "i") window of an Amtrak Train. Relax…as you see <u>tremendous</u> (stress "men") mountains…and <u>gentle</u> (softly) streams. And explore cities and towns and sights so <u>big</u> (say it big) and beautiful (say it with meaning)…they…take…your <u>breath</u> away."

Notice how the rate of speech changes at the end of the sentence. We slow it down to increase the impact of the statement.

And don't forget to say the word "breath" using only your breath, like it was meant to be said. The words "they take your" and "away" can be said with normal loudness, although emphasized individually.

When you get to the word *breath*, drop your loudness and almost whisper the word, making it *breathy*.

The Power of Paralinguistics

What is the power of paralinguistics? Can you describe someone who has "personality" using only nonverbal signals? How about someone with "charisma?" A lot of their charisma comes from their voice.

What are the voice elements of someone who is confident or credible? What do you think when you hear someone with a "smiling" voice. You probably like them right away.

Can you tell when someone is "talking down" to you? Their sentences end on a down note, or an abrupt note. They display the negative elements of paralinguistics. I can't believe the amount of businesses I call that have a receptionist who sounds like they're being burdened by your phone call. I mean huge companies, who spend untold amounts of advertising dollars telling people they are friendly and credible, only to have receptionists (who offer the first impression of the company) sound unfriendly, even downright nasty! These companies don't understand the importance of paralinguistics in communication.

When you run a radio or television ad, it isn't enough to write salient copy. And it isn't enough to place your ad right in front of your potential audience. The copy needs to be delivered comfortably, confidently, in a relaxed pattern of communication that we're used to hearing when we are listening to a friend or authority. If we hear someone "reading" to us, we won't be drawn to what is being said. That can be a big waste of your advertising dollars.

AdSense not only involves the way we think about advertising and marketing, it involves the words we use to express our message and the <u>way</u> we express the words paralinguistically.

When you once get a person's full attention, then is the time to accomplish all you ever hope with them. Cover every phase of your subject. One fact leads to some, one to another. Omit any one and a certain percentage will lose the fact which might convince. In one reading of an advertisement, one decides for or against a proposition.

--Claude Hopkins

Chapter Eighteen
The Message—Writing Effective Ad Copy

So how should you write effective copy for the micro-advertiser? It is, of course, a rhetorical question. There are so many factors to consider.

What kind of business do you have? That's very important to know. You write copy differently for each type of business.

What is your competition doing? Are they aggressive or passive? Are there many of them, or just one or two? Do you want to dominate, or just compete? This is where positioning comes into play.

What is your location relative to your competitors? What are the advantages you have over your competitors? The disadvantages?

If there is a distinct, recognizable disadvantage, it should be addressed in the message.

Remember, with consistency the public will believe your message...eventually. Take the Toyota dealer who ranked in about the middle of the pack in retail sales among 12 Toyota dealers in a major market. His ad campaign focused on one consistent element. The General Manager, who did his own spots, said in every ad "We're going to be #1 soon."

He developed a multi-media campaign including billboards, radio and television. And in every single ad he claimed his aspiration. He didn't say "we <u>want</u> to be #1." He said "we're <u>going</u> to be #1 soon."

Within a year, he was well on his way. Only one problem, though. He kept the campaign going too long. After 5 years of saying "we're going to be #1 real soon," the public caught on that they never <u>were</u> going to be #1! And he never was.

Or take my example earlier of the Dodge dealer who proclaimed himself "Atlanta's Dodge Giant!" The smallest dealer lot in town became Atlanta's Dodge giant within a year.

Did you notice in both examples that it took a year? Remember realistic expectations? A lot of businesses have written copy points such as these and kept it up for 2 or 3 months. They get frustrated because business hasn't turned around and they change direction. And they lose a lot of money in residual effect.

I handle the advertising for the nation's largest floor covering store, Carpets of Dalton in Dalton, Georgia...the carpet capitol of the world. For over six years, they used Don Sutton, the great Atlanta Braves sports announcer and Hall of Fame pitcher, as their on-camera spokesperson.

About the time I took over the account, we quit using him. Several years later, I was still hearing "Oh, that's the carpet store that

Don Sutton talks about.

Residual effect can be tremendous, but it takes a lot of time and money to build that residual.

Swaying the public takes time, money and patience. Especially if you have nothing better than rhetoric to distinguish yourself from your competitor. Even, as we said earlier, if the rhetoric is true!

Every commercial needs three elements…an attention getter, a salient point and a call to action.

First you must determine your desired end result. Then define your salient point.

For example, if the desired end result is for someone to pick up the telephone and call your number, the salient point would be your phone number.

Consider advertising you see for personal injury attorneys. The legal communities and the advertising communities look down on it as "schlock" advertising, but that's their elitist opinion.

It is a profession. And a very competitive one. Just look in your yellow pages for the personal injury attorney near you. They're as plentiful as convenience stores!

Why is it considered demeaning to the legal profession to run an ad for a personal injury attorney on television during a daytime soap opera? You'd have to ask an attorney.

Why do P.I. attorneys do it? Because it makes good marketing sense, and it is the most cost-effective way for them to advertise. Let's analyze the salient audience.

Who would call a P.I. attorney? First, it would be someone who has either been injured in a serious accident, or knows someone who has. These are the only people who would potentially respond to this message on any given day.

Second, it would be a person injured in an accident who is sitting in front of a television. That makes sense too. If they're seriously injured, they are somewhere recuperating. The television is usually right there.

That's why daytime television makes sense. It is one of the least expensive day-parts, and television has a captured audience.

Finally, the people who respond to P.I. advertising are primarily low middle to middle class citizens. That is television's primary audience.

So we've identified our salient audience, and our end result... to pick up the phone. From there it's easy to describe the salient message.

"If you've been injured in an accident, call this number."

Any attempt to stray away from this method will result in an increased opportunity for failure.

If you've ever watched daytime television in most markets, you will see an abundance of attorney ads. And they all have the same basic message. "If you've been injured in an accident, call this number." So how do you get your message to stand out?

You do it by "dressing up" the salient point. This is where the creativity comes in.

There are many talented, creative copywriters in the world. But you must be talented and creative after you have developed your salient point and determined your desired end result. Otherwise, your ad might win awards but fail to get adequate results. It's like being all dressed up with no place to go!

So what are some tips for "dressing up" your message so it will stand out? Here are some suggestions.

One way is to brand your business with a recognizable music bed. I don't mean a silly jingle that sounds like it was produced in the 1960s. You know the ones I'm talking about, the ones with the *Ray*

Conniff Singer sound-a-likes, singing...

> *We'll treat you special,*
> *We'll treat you like friends...*
> *From our service to our*
> *sales,*
> *We'll follow the trends.*
> *Get the best deal today*
> *From your friendly Ford*
> *dealer...*
> *Joe Smith Ford,*
> *On Broadview at Peeler!*

Yuck! No, don't waste your money on that. Your music doesn't even need words. Just a good, dynamic music bed that the public hears every time they listen to your ad.

And make sure the music compliments the delivery. If your message is urgent, use urgent music. If your message is placid, use appropriate music.

Find a recognizable, consistent voice. I can always tell when I hear a movie promo for a Disney film. You know the voice I'm talking about. That friendly, sincere, unthreatening voice introducing "the exploits of seven unforgettable dwarfs and the beautiful Show White."

Avoid trying to tell the audience your entire story in 60 seconds. Remember, the audience isn't there to listen to your ads. If you haven't caught their attention in the first 3 seconds, you've <u>lost</u> their attention.

Don't try to reach everyone with one message. Department store newspaper ads are a good example. They will run a full page ad promoting a storewide one-day sale, but the ad will show a woman or two in casual dresses, promoting the junior miss department.

What about the men's department, or fragrances, or jewelry or housewares? A department store has something for everyone, but the ads focus on only one point. Believe me, the public gets the idea. They'll be drawn to the store by knowing it's a one day event, and they'll pass all those other departments on the way to the junior miss department.

Laundry listing, as it is known, is effective for tire stores and grocery sale days, because people are perusing those ads for a specific purpose.

Don't try to tell your entire story. Just tell enough to get the public's interest. If you do that effectively, they'll take the effort to find out more. The purpose of advertising is <u>not</u> to tell someone everything they need to know about your business or service. The purpose is simply to get them to your phone or your door. The selling starts when they get there. One of the biggest reasons why 85% of advertising doesn't work is because micro-advertisers think they have to get as many points across as they can. After all, they're paying for all that time or space, so they want to fill it!

I discourage my clients from putting street addresses in their radio ads. It is wasting valuable seconds, and the people driving around in their cars can't write down the address. Give them a recognizable landmark. They'll find you, <u>if</u> you've done your job in the copy and given them a reason to respond in the first place.

If you don't have an easily recognizable phone number, don't use it. People know how to find your number, if you've gotten their interest.

Even in print ads you shouldn't give away too much information. People have a tendency to fill every available inch of the ad they are paying for. But an ad with a lot of white space usually attracts your eyes.

The print ad should be visually appealing to your audience. Notice how quick and simple it is to divert your eyes from this page you are reading. Once the eyes are diverted in the newspaper, the prospect is lost.

If every other ad is cluttered, and most of them are, just imagine how yours will stand out if it <u>isn't</u> cluttered.

Over the years, I assigned students of mine the task of writing a 60 second radio ad. The topics varied, the delivery varied, but over 90% of the time, one thing was constant. Most of them tried to fill the entire 60 seconds with words. That's a natural tendency. It's easy to write 60 seconds worth of copy and slap some music behind it. But to be creative, you must go "outside the box."

Chic-fil-A, the successful Atlanta based fast food franchise, developed a great campaign "outside the box." They utilized billboards, a one-dimensional medium with definite size parameters.

Their message was cute. They used cows painting the billboard with catch phrases like "Eat More Chicken." And they always spelled a word or two wrong.

The trick, though, was to actually construct life-size cows, climbing up ladders and holding paintbrushes, suggesting they had just painted the sign. That is being "outside the box!"

Don't try to fill your box with too much information. For instance, in radio ads, use sound effects to separate or reinforce the words. Radio is called "theater of the mind." The opportunity to create <u>any</u> scenario is endless.

In writing ads, use your creativity. But don't leave out the element of salience. Don't rely on rhetoric. Find your salient audience, and determine the one or two things that will draw them in. Then package it in something that will get their attention.

Don't try to reinvent the wheel. Most new ideas are not new, they are borrowed! They just have different packaging.

A lot of micro-advertisers who buy radio or television will let the station personnel write the ads. That is fine, because a lot of them are very creative. They just don't understand the behavioral science of advertising. They are usually young rookies in the business, unless you are buying a major station in a major market. Let them write the ads, but before they produce it, look at the copy. Make sure the spot is defining a specific audience with a specific message. Otherwise, you'll have a spot that doesn't work.

If you want to make your ad dollars work, use the elements of AdSense to write your copy, unless it is just a "branding" message. Then all you need is the creativity.

Advertisement is the lubricant for the free enterprise system.

--Lee Arthur Keimenson

Chapter Nineteen
The Future of Advertising

The future of advertising for the micro-advertiser looks dim. Sources of media increase almost proportionately to the rise in media costs. As the global village grows, our avenues to information and entertainment become more abundant. Unfortunately our population isn't growing at nearly the same rate as this avalanche of information.

And on top of all this began the computer age. It snuck up on the baby boom generation, with one of its own changing the world. Bill Gates brought the world into everyone's home with his Microsoft. Suddenly, almost overnight, every corner of the world…sources of knowledge, sources of information, sources of people and places… were at our fingertips, in a way that was faster and more abundant than we've ever known in our history.

The small businesses that must survive in this over-communicated society are engulfed by more competition, rising media costs, and by the dilemma of how to reach their audience.

Why are media costs rising so much? The cost of a television ad in the 6 o'clock news in most markets has increased by nearly 400% in the decade of the 1990s. Radio ad costs grew at the same rate. Newspaper rates have increased by about 200% during the same period, while the circulation has decreased.

In addition, as our economy grows, and as the world of business changes, salaries increase. Costs of living increase. Unemployment has decreased, which puts more disposable income into the economy.

Following this flow, all the people who work in the media business are earning much more than they were a decade earlier. Today, mega-corporations are acquiring every radio and television station they can gobble up.

This phenomenon really began in the 1970s. The entrepreneurs of media foresaw a way to make small fortunes by selling these stations to the highest bidders. When the stations were purchased, the new owners would put them back on the auction block and nearly double or triple their profits within a few years.

This turnover continued at a torrid pace until about 1990, when the huge corporations and public companies were ready to pounce with the really <u>big</u> money. Imagine the debt service! Today, the cost of maintaining these operations is very forbidding. And advertising is <u>still</u> the only source of revenue. It is little wonder that media rates have increased so much.

In addition, newspaper circulations have declined dramatically in just about every market in the country. Local newscasts have also shown a dissatisfaction among viewers. According to a national survey by Insite Media Research, 22 percent of adults completely avoid local TV news, about double from the number ten years ago.

And now…the Internet! A computer in most American homes will take time away from the formerly exclusive sources of advertising information. Advertisers are taking their message to cyberspace in hopes of capturing audiences.

What impact will this have on the potential results of radio, television and newspaper advertising? The businesses that must advertise to capture their share of the marketplace will have to be more innovative and aggressive.

How aggressive should the survivors be? I recently heard a story about a college football game ending on a bad call. A defender went for an interception in the end zone and it was ruled a turnover. Television instant replay clearly showed that the ball hit the ground first, but the defender put on an award winning show. He knew the ball hit the ground, but the referee didn't see it. And college football does not use instant replay in disputed calls. Unfortunately, for the opposing team, it was a game-ending play.

The host of a radio talk show where I heard the story posed the question of whether there was a boundary between gamesmanship and ethics. It is an interesting question.

At what point in the heat of battle does fairness have to set in? I surmise that professional sports are played as a war. What is fair in war? Did the dropping of the atomic bomb on Hiroshima to end World War II go beyond the bounds of fairness?

Business is like war too. If 65% of all businesses fail within five years, what can an entrepreneur do to fight off the competition, survive and grow…within legal bounds? Should businesses put on kid's gloves for fear of overstepping the rules of competition?

The survival of the fittest <u>should</u> be the rule in the business world. If you do not go into business with the attitude and the commitment to be successful at the expense of smaller competitors, you should expect to follow a rugged road.

The computer age will change the landscape of the playing field for the players in the survival of the fittest. The lower and middle classes and the minorities who are now placed lower in the caste system will be better able to compete in the global marketplace. No one can see them. They can only see their intellect, which is determined by the way they communicate on a keyboard.

Advertising in the future will direct consumers to a web page, which will in turn have to convince a skeptic.

We are skeptics because we are assaulted by the rhetoric of advertising and are constantly disappointed by the product or service we are lured to. We feel duped by the words, and are more cautious the next time we hear them.

As I mentioned earlier, once you have determined the actual response you want to elicit from your ad, you have a limited space or time frame in which to accomplish your goal. The maximum space you have in print is the size of the ad you buy. The more space you need to explain your service or product, the more expensive it gets.

A radio or television spot has to convince us to respond in 30 or 60 seconds.

Now, all you have to do with your advertising is to simply direct someone to a web page. That can be done easier in a 30 second or 60 second ad. It doesn't take that much time or space to do this effectively.

The advertising geniuses of the future will be the designers of the web pages…the ones who tease you, through the simplicity of words, pictures and phrases, to get you to go beyond the home page and explore. You can sell your image, the advantages of your product or service, and even guide your audience into contacting you for more information…something that was nearly impossible to accomplish in 30 or 60 seconds. And this is a perfect way to build a client base.

What you do with your database can save you a lot of money on advertising, and keep you in touch with your target market on a personal basis. Of course, with the database you need your own website. With a database, you can learn your customer's preferences, when they buy and what they buy.

With a database of customers you have an accurate picture of the number of people who receive your message, you can count how many people respond to your message and you can measure the conversion rates of people who try free demos, order a sample, subscribe to your newsletter or buy your product.

When you have a good website up and running, you will need to manage it diligently to get the most effectiveness from it. You must promote it and get your potential customers to provide the necessary information so you can stay informed about them, their lifestyles and habits. You can customize the experience of your on-line presentation to specific psychographics.

Once this is done, you can save on printing and postage while keeping your clients informed. The huge expense of these major advertising revenue sources will be eliminated by a simple click.

The other entrepreneurs of advertising will be the ones who know how to get potential consumers to your web page…the keyboard kids with the corporate connections.

Buying products and services will become commonplace on the Internet as e-commerce, a term never before used in the history of economic expansion, suddenly becomes the king- maker.

But how will we determine which product or service to use as we swim through a myriad of choices in the waves of the web? The information we receive will continue to be important in our choices, but the basic nature of advertising will remain…image *is* everything!

And the images are still created by mass media.

Will the nature of shopping change, leaving us with a vast wasteland of mall cemeteries on deserted lots, and strip centers decaying in the suburbs? You can now do all your grocery shopping without leaving your home. Will this be the end of supermarkets as we know them?

The answer is no. It is a basic human need to interact on a social level. The malls and movie theaters and grocery stores are still the town squares of our society.

To get people to your website, you still need mass media. You might have the best web site in the world, but if no one knows about it, it is like being all dressed up with no place to go. A recent study of on-line brokers showed that it cost $200 to $300 to reach a customer through advertising, but it cost $1300 to get a customer by buying out other on-line brokerage companies.

People must find you, and they must want to come back to your home page. Get people to your web site through your advertising image, and let the information on the page reinforce the image.

E-commerce will definitely have an effect on retail shopping. To what extent is hard to say. It depends on the nature of the business.

In the waterbed wars of the 1980s, many young entrepreneurs

became wealthy through the benefits of sleeping on water. But in the late 1980s, the war ended and only the strong survived. That is because only about 20% of us desire to sleep on a flotation device…period! The other 80% want to keep sleeping the way they have always slept.

So when the waterbed market reached its critical mass, no amount of advertising could change the *creature of habit.*

There will be a critical mass of e-buyers too. I believe automobile purchases will account for about 20% of the retail business within eight years, but probably won't go beyond that point.

Humans still want to smell the new car showroom, negotiate with the salespeople and kick the tires. They will still desire to walk the lot and make a choice. And that will continue for as long as free enterprise allows negotiability.

For products or services that are less negotiable, the Internet will capture a larger share of the business.

Music stores and book stores, for instance, will suffer somewhat because it might be cheaper to order through the Internet. But you will still have to wait a few days for your product to get to your mailbox.

Products that are influenced by spontaneity, like books and music, will still need retail outlets to satisfy the nature inherent in all of us to "get it now." We are an impatient society, spoiled by years of wealth and instant gratification.

I recently had a conversation with one of my radio reps in Atlanta. He worked for a small Christian music station. He deals with small businesses, primarily. He told me the biggest objection he faced in calling on these businesses was that the owners refused to grow.

"At least 75% of my business is regular business," one merchant told him. "I'll always have them, so I don't need to advertise for more."

I told my rep to ask him his client if he was happy with his income. If you get a client who is truly happy with the income they produce, there's not a lot you can do to get him to spend any money fishing for new customers. But, I'm not sure you will find too many small businesses who do not want to grow their business.

Do not be satisfied with the base of customers you have. Competition could move in around the corner, and you could be in trouble. People's habits change. You need to invest in growing new customers.

Make sure the expectations are realistic. Remember, Budweiser spends millions of dollars a year on advertising. Most of Budweiser's business comes from people who already like the taste of Bud. Those millions of dollars are spent on the small increases Budweiser will get by adding new fans. The residual of the advertising will benefit the Bud drinkers by reinforcing their decision. It may appear that you are spending too much money to make new customers, but new customers are essential for survival in today's overcrowded retail business environment.

In order for the small businesses to survive, they must have an understanding of AdSense. If we are bombarded with up to 1500 messages a day now, it could increase to nearly 2500 messages with the addition of new mediums and increased opportunities.

The micro-advertisers will diminish with time as large, powerful public companies devour the marketplace and the minds of the consumer.

Here is some advice. For the remainder to survive, you must determine the <u>purpose</u> of your advertising. Decide on the end result, the behavioral response you want to elicit through your advertising dollars. Don't waste your money on messages that don't have a call to action.

Learn to <u>position</u> your product. Learn and understand the marketing plan of your competitors. Base your journey toward success on realistic expectations.

Understand what it will take to achieve success, and hold on to that success.

If you solicit expertise and advice, choose your counselors wisely. Don't just look at their awards. Look at their ability to get you <u>results</u>.

Get your head out of your ads if you don't understand AdSense. More than one aspiring entrepreneur have failed when they let their egos control their destiny.

Understand the strengths and weaknesses of all the media available to you. Use AdSense in determining your media buy. Don't allow the media to use your advertising dollars to fill holes. Remember, if an ad falls in the forest and there is no one around to hear it, it is questionable that a noise is made.

Learn how to add salience to your marketing. Identify your salient audience, and your salient point. If the message is aimed at the audience, your chance for success increases.

Avoid the rhetoric that has engulfed our advertising vocabulary. Understand that the public has become immune to it. The messages have become redundant, rhetorical and resilient. This is a combination that will lead to failure.

All this is easier said than done. But learn to think and plan as a behavioral scientist and you will be a step ahead of the other survivors.

The nature of advertising is indeed changing, because the nature of commerce is changing. And it is changing in whirlwind proportions.

Who could have predicted in 1950 that the average home would have nearly 100 choices in television stations by 1980? Who could have predicted in 1950 that the average American would have access to every corner of the world by 1980? And all at the click of a button in the comfort of their home.

And who can predict the possibilities in the year 2050? Will malls and movie theaters, grocery stores and car lots, become extinct? Where will the work force migrate? And what will happen to our social skills as we decrease our social exposure?

The future is in the hands of the cyber generation. These entreprencurs must allow us to progress cautiously and deliberately to our destiny. The consequences of their failure could cause a lot of turmoil, as well as heartache, in our society.

Social and economic collapse could be the result. AdSense will allow us to survive as a business community. Common sense will allow us to survive as a society.

ABOUT THE AUTHOR

Kirk Donovan is a veteran of over 30 years in advertising. He started at the bottom, literally, on-the-air and selling advertising for a 250 watt AM station in Niceville, Florida. Over the next 10 years, he worked his way through small market radio on the way to a Master's Degree and PhD studies in Behavioral Science at Florida State University. He learned along the way that the purpose of advertising was to get a response!

AdSense is a look at the behavioral science of advertising, from a veteran who learned the business on the streets and battled his way to the top.

Kirk owns one of the most successful advertising consulting firms in the country, and is a champion for the retailer who struggles through advertising decisions and wastes money along the way. He is one of the most sought-after speakers in the country on the Behavioral Science of Advertising. He has helped dozens of retailers take their businesses from zero to hero.

Printed in the United States
71117LV00004B/139-150